Love Is On the Move

Love for God. Love for Self. Love for Others.

Edited by **DENA CRECY**

As a married couple of 39 years, we strive every day to outdo each other with love, while understanding that the right way is not our way but God's way. What we've seen in Jeannette, in spite of experiencing relational griefs and disappointments, she still strives as an educator—not only in the public schools but in the spiritual lives of countless men and women, sharing God's Love in biblical truth within the many ministries she's involved in.

Gerald and Mary Whitfield

"Strength and dignity are her clothing, and she smiles at the future" (Proverbs 31:25). **The Love for God** is very informative in helping us experience and navigate the real love that the Father has for us. As we are well aware, the most challenging times are when we need to know and experience the genuineness of God's unconditional love for us. As we reflect on God's grace, we are assured that our relationship will be strengthened and gracefully fashioned as the Lord works according to his Divine Plan for our lives. Readers will get a clearer vision of life's challenges and regardless of what they may face in their personal lives, this will enlighten them to wait patiently and trust God's timing.

Debra Epps, Assistant Pastor of The Living Christ Church
Tulare, California

This book is exactly what every believer and non-believer should read. Love is truly the key ingredient in everything that we do, and most importantly, Love is who Jesus is.
Love is patient, love is kind, it is not jealous; love does not brag, it is not arrogant. It does not act disgracefully, it does not seek its own benefit; it is not provoked, does not keep an account of a wrong suffered, it does not rejoice in unrighteousness, but rejoices with the truth; it keeps every confidence, it believes all things, hopes all things, endures all things (1 Corinthians 13:4–7).

Kim Miller, Serves as a Head Usher at West Coast Believers Center
International, Visalia, California

In every relationship, mutual love, respect, and support are some of the key ingredients to success. Love is the cornerstone in sickness, wellness, and despair. Without the trusted love of Christ, family, and friends, the relationship may not thrive. To have a healthy couple's relationship, it takes the divine love of God shown in both individuals. God demonstrates love towards us in 1 Corinthians 16:14, "All that you do must be done in love." Modeling the love of Christ takes the ingredients in 1 Corinthians 13:4–6, "Love is patient, love is kind, it is not jealous; love does not brag, it is not arrogant. It does not act disgracefully, it does not seek its own benefit; it is not provoked, does not keep an account of a wrong suffered, it does not rejoice in unrighteousness, but rejoices with the truth."

Genuine love requires conscientiousness in personal commitment to the Lord and the other person. The Christ-focused relationship begins with a centrality of two individuals to seek the Lord by obeying this scripture in Matthew 22:36–40, "You shall love the Lord your God with all your heart and with all your soul and with all your mind." The relationship will blossom and mature when God is in the center. What a fabulous book you ladies have written.

Dr. Ella L. Brown
Early Childhood Director, Interim Principal
Kingdom Collegiate Academies
Women's Minister at Oak Cliff Bible Fellowship Church

Foreword

My name is Marasha Blakley, a woman deeply rooted in faith, a devoted daughter, aspiring author, and ambitious entrepreneur. I am thrilled as the time arrives to immerse myself in the pages of the new anthology, *Love Is On the Move*. While the title may sound cliché, the profound insights shared within have allowed me to delve deep and contemplate the essence of love.

From heartache, sadness, joy, fire, and excitement, each author shares their deep personal thoughts. This anthology takes a deeper dive into the intricacies of love, distinguishing its true nature and dispelling misconceptions. It offers practical guidance on how to embody love for God, oneself, and others in various aspects of life. Through personal testimonies, each author shares their journey with love, advocating for emotional processing and growth. From heartache to joy, each author bares their soul, offering a spectrum of emotions and experiences.

Reflecting on the previous anthology, *Therefore, Forgive, Love and Rest*, which courageously revealed painful truths, I found inspiration for healing and progress in my journey. *Love is on the Move* presents diverse perspectives that resonate with anyone's experiences. My hope and prayer is that this book will enrich your life as it has enriched mine.

Marasha Blakley
MHSA

Contents

The Path of Love and Divine Favor

Ethelene A. Boyd

Everything that God is and has created is unified in love. Although many have gone before me on this road of love, there are moments when I feel completely alone.

Hebrews 10:14 reminds me to be Spirit-led and holy every day, and I believe the Holy Spirit is teaching me to obey Christ and show His love. The Scripture specifically says that Jesus' offering made you perfect, but the Holy Spirit's work in your life continues to make you holy. This happens one step at a time, as we daily obey Jesus and follow Him. The more you choose to obey Christ and say no to the allures of this world, the more you grow in holiness. Be Spirit-led and holy (Hebrews 10:14).

On February 18, 1968, my husband, Ronnie Hatchett, and I were startled out of our sleep by the sound of a train wreck. We had the oven on and open to help heat our frigid house located near a farming community in Crete, Nebraska. We noticed that the gas burning on the oven looked as if were turning blue. We were freshmen at Doane College. Our daughter, Gloria, who was four years old at the time, slept in a room adjacent. The sound of the train derailing caused my husband to quickly grab our daughter and shout out orders for me to follow him outside of the house before it exploded. Dangerous anhydrous ammonia gas was on board the train and had permeated through the air because of the spill. We had no idea we should turn the gas oven off, stay inside the house, and put towels under the door and other crevices in the house.

As I followed my husband out of the house, I felt a searing pain in my throat and lungs as I stepped outside into the white cloud of lethal gas. The accident took the lives of the train conductor, two hitchhikers, some neighbors, my husband, and our baby. Out of everyone who ventured outdoors during the accident, I was the sole survivor. I fell face-forward in the snow and this likely reduced the effects of the anhydrous ammonia gas. The fate of my life was uncertain due to the presence of the toxic gas in my body. The emergency workers had written me off in the hospital. God chose to keep my unborn daughter Tracy and myself alive even though the accident severely injured our vocal cords and lungs.

My doctor warned me to stay in the hospital, but I checked myself out so I could attend my husband Ronnie's and daughter Gloria's funeral in Chicago. I was so shocked that I sat quietly in the pews at the rear of the church. Because of the burns to my lungs, no one expected me to attend the funeral of my husband and daughter. My vocal cords were badly burnt, and I was afraid I would never be able to talk clearly again; everything I uttered sounded like a whisper.

A week after the funeral, I flew back to college. My roommate Loretta, who lived in the girls' dorm, pushed me to maintain my participation in extracurricular activities. Love kept me anchored even though I felt numb, like a walking zombie. As I was chatting with Loretta and a few other A.F.R.O. House girlfriends on our way home one day, I suddenly heard a rumbling roar! My companions and I sprinted across the bridge. Once we had caught our breath, I attempted to speak again, this time in the loudest whisper possible, but I heard the exact same noise. When my voice was recognized as the source of the booming roar, we all began to giggle. The return of my voice!

That outburst demonstrated that I could still speak, even though the anhydrous ammonia gas had a lasting impact on my vocal cords. I moved into married housing and gave birth to my daughter Tracy on July 18, 1968, six months after the accident. Members of the Doane College football team would take shifts to watch Tracy while I went to school. Both Tracy and I would have violent coughing fits and our voices were lower in pitch than many others, but I am grateful that God saved us. God helped me weather this terrible catastrophe and all the others that have come my way. His love has lifted me for my entire 75-plus years on this planet. I rejoice in God's love and choice blessings for me. Sharing the many lessons I have learned as a recipient of God's love is an honor and a privilege. I want to make sure to give God all the glory, honor, and praise.

What I've Learned About Loving God, Myself, and Other People

Lesson 1: Our devotion to God changes over time. I kept thinking about the vision I saw of my mom as I was lying face down in the snow after the accident. I reassured her, "Mama, you did good." I physically sensed that I could very well be near the end of my life on earth, and God offered me the option to either remain on earth and carry out my mission here or go to my heavenly home. So, I stayed. There was still life in me. The best way I can put it is that I had a spiritual awakening during this out-of-body experience. I came to a deeper connection with God and realized he was always there for me every minute, every second, and every moment. Nothing remained the same when I realized God was with me.

Lesson 2: Every age is welcome by God. As a three-year-old, I made the move to Chicago from Mississippi. It was around that time that my parents, Dora and Eugene, were married. We were met at the Chicago train station by the pastor of our new church. I recall attending revivals and tent meetings in Tupelo and Guntown every summer from the time I was five years old until I was thirteen years old when I rode the train back to Mississippi. To draw nearer to God, the ministers urged us to fast and pray. At the revival, I was astounded to hear my classmates speak in tongues. Is this what the gift of the Holy Ghost looked like, engaging in activities such as speaking in tongues, dancing, and handclapping?

"Oh, Lord, you haven't given me these unique abilities yet," I pondered.

I put my faith in Christ during the summer revival when I was around eight years old. God accepted me just the way I was and loved me for it. All he wanted was for me to be willing to serve. What was meant by being delivered, restored, and sold out to God? I had no idea. However, God reassured me that whether I could speak in tongues like the other kids my age or not, He still loved me and would provide instructions for me to live. God has comforted me and counseled me through the Holy Spirit. My faith has never been stronger ever since and God has shown me His signs and wonders throughout my life.

Lesson 3: Think on your life and how God is in control (sovereign) and protecting you. Around the time of Brown v. Board of Education in 1954, I began kindergarten in Chicago when I was five years old. The course of my experience was altered by this landmark. It seems like just yesterday I was walking to school with kids of my own race, and then the next thing I knew, I was trekking two or three miles each way to attend the more prestigious school with white students. A complete and utter systemic upheaval seemed to have taken place.

Thankfully, I was labeled as a college bound student who was planning to attend a university. When my mother told the school personnel that I was exceptionally bright and should be placed in gifted and talented classes, they simply believed her without extensive testing. I worked hard to prove my mom right when she said I was smart. I was essentially the third-ranked member of my 1968 graduating class in the group of students headed to college.

Lesson 4: Be prepared for the unexpected. Life is full of surprises, but God is never surprised. A neighbor's son raped me when I was 13 years old, and I became pregnant as a result. I have tried to erase most memories of the trauma. However, I do recall passing out from fumes while shopping with my mom at a paint store. My mom took me to the doctor and her suspicions were confirmed. She immediately went to our neighbor's house and talked to the boy's mom about this pregnancy. I had a lot of support from my mom and the boy's mom. I had the baby at age 14, and I let the boy's family name the baby. He said she resembled his sister who had passed away unexpectedly, so we named the baby Gloria in memory of his sister.

"Someone important is coming over," my mom told me when I was thirteen years old. I had no idea that my dad was different from my sisters' dad, who my mom married when I was three. Nonetheless, she informed me that she had spoken with my biological father, Mozelle Ezekiel, and that he would be seeing me soon. Without questioning or challenging anything, I merely accepted things as they were. The man I thought was my dad was good to me and I loved him, but this new discovery was a pleasant surprise.

The day I met my biological dad was one of the best days ever. I felt our connection and his love for me instantly. From that point on, every weekend I would ride the bus to Chicago's South Side. Every month, I would set aside a weekend to spend with him, just the two of us. Sometimes we'd even go out to restaurants. The friends he introduced me to were always very kind and accepting. My dad had given me a special watch; it quickly became my most treasured item, a constant reminder that the Lord's love is unending is found in Lamentations 3:22–23. God knew that I had a different father from the one I thought I had. God was there at the precise moment I needed Him most, at this crossroads in my life.

Lesson 5: Take advantage of unique opportunities and God's favor. Throughout my high school career, I was blessed to be a part of a program called Upward Bound. It was truly a Godsend in terms of preparing me for college. We would go and reside in the dorms of Northwestern University in Evanston, Illinois each summer. While there, we would acquire new study skills and gain insight into living a life completely different from our usual ones. We got a stipend, opened bank accounts, and regularly had wonderful experiences, such as visiting operas and sailing on a boat. We went to special shows, wrote, and put on plays that we directed and performed in.

During my last summer at Upward Bound, I had the opportunity to co-direct *Alice in Wonderland* with Daphne Maxwell Reid, who is famous for her role as the second Vivian Banks on the NBC sitcom *Fresh Prince of Belair*. Another highlight of my time being involved in college bound activities was meeting my first husband, Ronnie Hatchett, in a high school production of *Green Acres*. He was a star alongside me in our production that featured the acting talents of the whole football squad. My co-star ended up becoming my spouse.

Lesson 6: Pray, pray, pray. As a teenager in Chicago, I remember lounging on a patio overlooking Sacramento Boulevard. On the porch, I spent every day praying and contemplating. Sitting on the terrace, I said, "God, if you love me and use me, I will be so grateful that I will spend the rest of my life serving you." Looking back, I see how everything that followed was a blessing from God. Everything is happening for my good, even though my life isn't always perfect (Romans 8:28). I decided to drop out of high school, take the GED exam, and join my husband, Ronnie, at college early because I wanted a better life for our child. I could go to college and take my family out of what some called "The Ghetto" on the west side of Chicago.

Lesson 7: Never stop learning. Recalibrate. Relaunch. Even though the accident was a horrible experience, I persisted. After Ronnie died, I became closer to one of his Doane football teammates, Willie Owens. We married, and he embraced my daughter Tracy as his own. We welcomed a son whom we affectionately called "Chip." Unfortunately, Chip died from sudden infant death syndrome a few months after birth. Every new day is an opportunity to hug, hold, and share your unconditional love with those you care about. You never know when the last time you will be able to hold your loved ones. I graduated from Doane College after finishing my student teaching assignment. In my never-ending desire to become an exceptional instructor, I studied hard. I put my abilities to use in a variety of ways. I greatly enjoyed being an unconventional teacher and dealing with 30 to 40 extraordinarily gifted first graders each school year. Before retiring, I was awarded with the 2007 Doane College Excellence in Teaching Award and the Davenport Community School District's Golden Apple Award. For a time, I held positions of leadership in both the National Education Association and the Iowa State Council of Education. In later years, I served as the church's financial secretary and a member of the Civil Rights Commission.

Lesson 8: Rely on others when you're weak. Work-life balance is a constant issue when raising children and serving in ministry. I had the resources to hire a maid, which helped me stay organized and retain my equilibrium. I learned not to be afraid of decluttering. Now, when I come across an item in my home that does not bring me joy, I remind myself to let it go. Traveling and participating in things that I enjoy are top considerations for me. I had the opportunity to help raise not only my own children, but also those of my sisters. One of my life goals was to raise kids so that they would regard themselves as capable of pursuing their deepest aspirations and callings, becoming household leaders and change agents in their communities and nations. I pray that they will be happy and healthy disciples of Jesus Christ. The notion of teaching a youngster in the right path serves as a guiding light for me (Proverbs 22:6).

Lesson 9: To be a blessing who can bless others, pray that the Holy Spirit will guide your spiritual development. If someone helped you develop, don't be shy about saying thanks. However, keep in mind that you are obligated to reciprocate. Join forces with other believers who are passionate about Christ. Always team up with like-minded individuals who are on fire for Christ. God places people in your life to keep encouraging you. Keep running this Christian race and help others get closer to God.

My pastor in Davenport, Iowa, Rev. Rogers Kirk Jr., was asked to preach internationally for a revival. The pastor asked me how to pronounce the name of the country he would visit. This simple question prompted the revelation of my future calling. God used me to help plan this mission trip and help organize the mission team. I checked out twelve books from the Davenport Public Library to place in the church hallway so members of the church would know just where our mission team was going and the need for worldwide missions. I did my best to help Pastor Kirk get his passport and make his travel as smooth as possible. He extended the invitation for me to travel to Liberia to teach the women and the children at the revival. The weight of this obligation originally scared me. I accepted that God was using me in this new way. This responsibility of winning souls for Christ was profound. God trusted me to share His word and he helped me do it through artistic endeavors.

Lesson 10: International teaching and service is an honor. I have doubted my abilities on occasion, but God assures me that with Him, I am capable of all things (Philippians 4:13). If you feel like you are called to travel overseas to share the gospel, just analyze your gifts, get with a team, and do it. My old self believed that to be useful to the master, I had to adopt another person's traits. One preacher, Rev. Snowden, who is a regular at our Zoom Bible study, really struck me as remarkable. The pastor was so impressed by her oratory skills that he invited her to the pulpit on her visit last year. I could envision her as a church leader since her voice was crystal clear and she knew her stuff when it came to the Bible. I was reminded by the Holy Spirit that God utilizes every one of us in our own unique way. My church family had a service recognizing me as Missionary Boyd. This showed me that I was enough. Philippians 4:6 reminds us: "Be anxious for nothing, but in everything by prayer and supplication with thanksgiving let your requests be made known to God."

Lesson 11: Love-based partnerships are valuable. I've been blessed to be one of nineteen missionaries who go to Zambia twice a year with a team from Mt. Hebron Missionary Baptist Church in Garland, Texas. We build schools and train teachers in Zambia. My trips have been financially challenging, but God has placed it on the hearts of others to support several of my mission trips.

Lesson 12: Your words, thoughts, and deeds will reflect your love for God and your devotion to studying His Word. Give yourself up to God and allow Him to shape you into His image bearer. The question, "Where would the body be if they were all one part?" is asked in 1 Corinthians 12:19–23: "There are many members, but one body. And the eye cannot say to the hand, 'I have no need of you,' nor again the head to the feet, 'I have no need of you.' No, much rather, those members of the body which we think to be less honorable, on these we bestow greater honor, and our unpresentable parts have greater modesty."

Lesson 13: Collaborate with individuals who share your vision for the kingdom. I had the privilege of visiting my friend Venus in Chicago, who I met while involved with Upward Bound. During our visit, I witnessed a ministry team outside the Illinois courthouse praying, handing out brochures, and encouraging people to repent, believe, and trust God. The majority of people wanted prayer. After their trial, many testified that the prayers had an impact, either on the outcome of the case or on their own behavior. Upon returning to Davenport, I shared my experience with Pastor Kirk regarding my time at Venus' church in Chicago. The pastor then had me invite leaders of her church to visit our team in Iowa, and we followed their lead, introducing Courtside Ministries to the Quad City, Iowa community.

Lesson 14: It's alright to feel what you're feeling. Ask the Holy Spirit to fill you up. Psalm 23 reminds me that God wants me to rest. It's alright to feel down sometimes. It's alright to go to therapy. It's okay for me to take advantage of solitude sometimes. After benediction at church, I would often leave without having a long conversation with people. I felt guilty for not wanting to fellowship. I accept that my personality changed due to a car accident that injured my brain and caused a concussion. I rarely mention it, but I had trouble remembering and communicating. When I'm running on empty, I sometimes stay in bed. I have learned to be gentle with myself. If I feel myself sinking into a depression, I have learned to encourage myself in the Lord.

"Love is on the move" means God is working in us and through us in many ways. Right now, there are days when I feel like I can manage things on my own and days when my life feel like it's out of control. I accept that I am getting older and it is okay to want to take life at a more relaxed pace. It is most important for me to be around family and people who love me and mean the most to me.

Lesson 15: Stand on God's promise that your latter will be greater than your past. I am in the process of downsizing and decluttering my home in Iowa and moving to Allen, Texas with my daughter, Willene, and my son, Jon. Instead of feeling like I am not able to lead like I used to, I realize the scope of my responsibility has changed. It's time for me to enjoy the fruit of my labor and rest. I have poured out to others, and now others can pour into me. These are my latter days, and I am participating in this endeavor to express my gratitude to God.

My life has been filled with fascinating experiences, even though it may not be immediately apparent when meeting me for the first time. As I share my lessons learned on the path of love and God's favor, I am reassured that you will see that God has blessed and anointed my life. My devotion to God compels me to share how He has worked in my life. I can tell you about how He loved a girl from Chicago's West Side and used her to encourage others going through similar struggles.

I have triumphed over poverty and depression, and I am moving forward daily.

It is a daily commitment to press toward the mark for the prize of the high calling of God in Christ Jesus (Philippians 3:14). I continue trusting in God and studying His word. I had to teach myself that God's unconditional love and acceptance teaches me how to love and it is my responsibility to teach others how to love. When I was a child, I spoke as a child, I understood as a child, I thought as a child: but when I became an adult, I put away childish things (1 Corinthians 13:11).

"Love is on the move" means that God is working in us in various ways. Lately, I've felt like God wants me to study more. God is revealing His expectations for me in this new chapter. His pathway can be clear whether you are young and committed or whether you are old and considered a seasoned saint. I was young and now I am old. I have never seen the righteous forsaken, nor His seed begging bread (Psalm 37:25).

God is with us. God has ordered my steps on this path of love and favor. My life experiences and opportunities have shaped my praise and devotion to God. I am thankful to God for teaching me how to love myself and others. I am inspired to make a difference, and I celebrate when God makes a difference through me. I am grateful that God has allowed me to reflect on my past experiences because they have shown me that God has played a greater plan for my life than I could have ever dreamed. I still have much work to do, and my daily responsibility is to keep praying, studying, and committing myself to God's will.

I am on the path of love and divine favor. And love is on the move.

ABOUT

Ethelene A. Boyd

Ethelene A. Boyd is a 75-year-old retired educator. Some of her current involvements include serving as a Civil Rights Commissioner and leading the Courtside Ministry in Davenport, Iowa.

She has dedicated her life to uplifting others. She is described as a missionary who has dedicated her time, talent, and resources to travel to several countries in Africa to train teachers, promote education, and build schools.

She stands outside the courthouse with the Courtside Ministry to pray for those involved in legal proceedings.

For over 45 years, she shared her vision inside classrooms as an educator in the Davenport Community School District.

Her name is recorded in numerous history books for her legacy as a pioneering educator and dedicated instructor who received lifetime achievements, including The Golden Apple Award.

She is known as a respected elder in her community and is lovingly called "Mother Kwanzaa" for her work in sharing the unifying principles of Kwanzaa.

She joyfully spreads the good news about overcoming health challenges, the importance of good mental health, and regular therapeutic care. She is recognized for her efforts to engage with her community in dialogue about diabetes, turning around kidney disease, ADHD, and depression. She is known for her kindness and generosity towards everyone she meets. She now enjoys traveling and visiting her kids, her grandchildren, and great grandchildren as well as participating in cultural events to inspire the community.

> "Serve the Lord with jubilation; come before Him with rejoicing."
>
> Psalm 100:2

Love: The Superior Way

Dena Crecy

Introduction

T he word "love" has become so common that the meaning has been diluted. We say love for just about everything. For example, "I love a particular type of food, I love a certain type of hair style, I love the color blue, I love that movie, I love that song, I love that book, I love my job, I love my family, and I love him or her."

In some foreign countries, they are amused at how we use the word love in America. They have specific words that describe the type of love they are referencing. In Norwegian: *Jeg elsker deg*—I love you. This phrase has a much deeper meaning than in English. This isn't something you say to your friend. It's used when one has very deep feelings of love toward their partner, so never use it lightly. *Jeg liker deg*—I like you. This is a casual phrase that is often used with friends. *Jeg er glad i deg*—I like you very much, or I am very fond of you. This phrase is more intimate than "Jeg liker deg." It's normally used between family members and close friends. When I heard this expressed, it got me thinking about the various ways I use the word love. This information has caused me to be more intentional about how I used the word love and pray you will also.

Why This Project?

My goal with this writing is to share how Love is still on the move—Love for God, Love for Self, Love for Others—using the Bible as a point of reference. There are four types of love the Bible refers to:

1. Agape, which is unconditional love. It's the kind of love that God has for us (John 3:16) and the kind of love He wants us to have for one another (John 13:35).

2. Storage, which is family love. This is the love that exists between family members (Ruth and Naomi, Ruth 1:16–17), (Mary and Jesus, John 19:25–27), and close friendships (David and Jonathan, 1 Samuel 18:1–3).

3. Next is Phileo, which is brother love. It's a love that is built on mutual respect, trust and shared values. There is a beautiful description in Proverbs 17:17. Another example is Jesus and His disciples in John 15:15. It is also evident in the early Christian community in Acts 2:42–47. Brotherly love shows up in the good and the bad, as we see in Galatians 6:2, where we are admonished to bear one another burdens.

4. The last of the four kinds of love in the Bible is Eros—romantic love. This is the passionate and romantic love that exists between two people who are deeply attracted to one another. The Bible's examples are with a man and a woman. While Eros love can be a beautiful and powerful force, it's important to remember that it should be experienced within the context of a committed, God-centered relationship, such as marriage. Some examples are Adam and Eve (Genesis 2:23–

24) and Song of Solomon (Solomon 8:6–7). It is also worth noting that, in the context of the Bible, Eros love is not only about physical attraction but also about a deep emotional and spiritual connection between two people as stated in Ephesians 5:25. This is the love I'm still believing God to receive on this side of heaven.

My Love for God

"We love, because He first loved us."
1 John 4:19

My introduction to the love of God came in Houston in 1984 when I heard the gospel of salvation in church shared and accepted the invitation to begin a relationship with Jesus Christ through that particular church. My eyes were opened to a whole new world, and it made sense to me. I was in my early 20s, married, and excited about this new journey with the Lord. My love for this new relationship grew as I was on fire for the Lord.

After a few years on this great journey, the enemy introduced himself—with a vengeance. The adultery door was swung wide open, and my marriage was under attack. I fought that battle for seven years, and then God said it was time to let it go. So, in July of 1995, I filed for divorce. I must admit, I was very disappointed with God, as I believed He could have fixed it. I was listening to the voice of the enemy telling me that God didn't love me and other things to torment me in an attempt to separate me from my faith. I had a pity party for a brief time. It was so bad that I couldn't even get out of bed. I'm thankful I was connected to and serving in church. A few of the women from the women's ministry I served with came by and wouldn't leave until I let them in. They made me get out of bed, shower, eat, and leave the house. It was their love and care, along with the word of God, that brought me back.

As I reflected on the trial, I was reminded of the many times that God showed up for me and my children in the midst of the fight. As I read the Bible and the many characters that had trials and tribulations, I realized that trials are a part of life. Jesus said in John 16:33, "I have said these things to you, that in me you may have peace. In the world you will have tribulation. But take heart; I have overcome the world." To read the details of what happened in my marriage, you can get a copy my book, *Therefore, Forgive, Love, and Rest* on Amazon. It focuses on forgiveness and God's love.

After being divorced for 5 years, God sent me to the DFW area through my employer. It was a fresh start, away from what was familiar and the heartaches in Houston. I have to admit, I thought by now I would be remarried. However, I have accepted God's plan for me, single or married, and I'm excited to continue to serve Him.

> "Jesus answered and said to him, 'If anyone loves Me, he will follow My word; and My Father will love him, and We will come to him and make Our dwelling with him.'"
>
> *John 14:23*

There have been many other trials and tribulations, like losing my mom, homelessness, and relationship disappointments, but my perspective and response have been different. I believe in the sovereignty of God.

Learning to love myself.

> "'Love the Lord your God with all your heart and with all your soul and with all your mind and with all your strength.' The second is this: 'Love your neighbor as yourself.' There is no commandment greater than these."
>
> *Mark 12:30–31*

I used to criticize myself all the time, even after coming to Christ. My hair is not right, boobs too big, hips too big, pug nose, big feet, gap in teeth (which I attempted to correct with four years of braces and wearing a retainer—worked for a while, then not). That came from the spirit of comparison, which I learned was a spirit. We tend to focus more on what we think is wrong with us than what is right.

Another thing about myself that used to annoy me is that people would regularly—I mean *regularly*—come up to me and say, "I think I know you," or, "You look familiar." I would look like their best friend, auntie, etc. It would always be someone positive in their life. My response would be, "You saw my face on the wall of the most wanted at the Post Office." It wasn't until I took part in a 12-week women's discipleship class in 1998 that came a reproof and correction from the Holy Spirit, through the Word, to stop saying that. Sometimes, to be corrected, we have to be in an environment to receive what the Word has to say to us at the time.

> "All Scripture is inspired by God and beneficial for teaching, for rebuke, for correction, for training in righteousness; so that the man or woman of God may be fully capable, equipped for every good work."
> *2 Timothy 3:16–17*

I learned that I was created on purpose, and that He has a wonderful plan for my life.

> "For You created my innermost parts; You wove me in my mother's womb. I will give thanks to You, because I am awesomely and wonderfully made; Wonderful are Your works, And my soul knows it very well."
>
> *Psalm 139:13–14*

> "For we are His workmanship, created in Christ Jesus for good works, which God prepared beforehand so that we would walk in them."
>
> *Ephesians 2:10*

I learned that when I complain about how I was made, it is saying to God that He didn't do it right or He didn't know what He was doing when He created me. I was created on purpose, for a purpose, and He "knit me together in my mother's womb." I also learned to recognize that God made me approachable and that can start a meaningful connection that could lead a person to Him. So, what did I do with this new knowledge or awakening?

In my research, I read a lot of articles on biblical love, as well as diving deep into what the scripture has to say about love, and found that according to the Bible, after our love for God, self-love is next. We cannot extend His love to others that we don't give to ourselves.

Of the articles I read, I like the one by Alonda Tanner, called, "Self-Love and Christianity," published in 2016. In it, she shares some ways to fiercely love yourself.

1. Value your identity in Christ.

God has a lot of inspiring things to say about you! Recognizing the truth about your identity in Christ is essential, but remember, who we are is all about Him! The identity He has given us is for His purpose and His glory—not solely ours. That, my friend, is when self-love becomes sinful—when we elevate ourselves above God. Check out some reminders below.

- I am a daughter of the King. (2 Corinthians 6:18)
- I am strong. (2 Corinthians 12:10)
- I am chosen. I am royalty. (1 Peter 2:9)
- I am loved. (John 15:9; Romans 5:8; Galatians 2:20)

2. Stop Comparing.

Seriously, you were made to stand out! You were made to be different! Even Dr. Seuss says, "Why fit in when you were born to stand out?" This is so important to understand, not just for your contentment, but for understanding how God intended the body of Christ to function. In his letter to the church in Corinth, Paul writes:

"For the body is not one part, but many. If the foot says, 'Because I am not a hand, I am not a part of the body,' it is not for this reason any less a part of the body. And if the ear says, 'Because I am not an eye, I am not a part of the body,' it is not for this reason any less a part of the body. If the whole body were an eye, where would the hearing be? If the whole body were hearing, where would the sense of smell be? But now God has arranged the parts, each one of them in the body, just as He desired. If they were all one part, where would the body be? But now there are many parts, but one body."

1 Corinthians 12:14–20

Your make-up, your skills, talents, strengths, weaknesses—they all belong. There is a specific need for *you* in the body of Christ. Don't abandon your peace by comparing yourself to others.

3. Nurture Your Relationship with God.

An older woman shared with me, "The most important thing in the world is a relationship with God through His son Jesus Christ." She wasn't lying. One of the best acts of love towards yourself is to spend time building your relationship with the Lord.

Start talking to Him. In Christian circles, this is called prayer, and it's as simple to begin as talking to a friend is. What's amazing is that God hears our prayers and because He loves us and wants a relationship with us, He responds to our prayers too, as stated in 1 John 5:14–15.

Read Your Bible. The best way to get to know God is through the pages of the Bible. The Bible helps us recognize the character of God, the things He loves, His priorities, and His hope for us. It trains us to recognize His voice so when He does respond to our prayers or when He reaches out to us (He does that!), we can recognize His voice. The more we study the Bible and the more we talk with and listen to the Lord, the closer we get to Him. An on-fire relationship with God *will* change your life.

4. Steward Your Strengths.

Every gift and talent that God has given you, He has given you for a purpose. That purpose extends far beyond our own ambitions and earthly gains. Do God things with the things God has given you. When you are able to recognize these things in yourself and grow in them, you typically become able to do the same for others: call out the good in them, speak into their strengths. There is a *free* spiritual gift assessment that the Teams Ministry sponsors at gifts.churchgrowth.org.

5. Take Care of Your Body.

We take care of the things we love, right? So, take care of yourself. Eat like you love your body, move like you love your body, and rest like you love your body. Be a good steward of yourself. In doing so, we model healthy self-care for others. Do you struggle with seeing your body the way God describes it? Use these Bible verses about caring for yourself to help you adopt God's perspective of your body and its purpose.

> "But now, Lord, You are our Father; we are the clay, and You our potter, and all of us are the work of Your hand."
>
> *Isaiah 64:8*

> "For no one ever hated his own flesh, but nourishes and cherishes it, just as Christ also does the church."
>
> *Ephesians 5:29*

> "Do you not know that you are a temple of God and that the Spirit of God dwells in you?"
>
> *1 Corinthians 3:16*

How do I know love myself? I am patient and kind to myself. I rest when I'm tired, and when I not. I have learned to say, "No," and that the word no is a complete sentence, meaning no explanation is required. I completely changed my eating habits in 2022 and began an exercise routine, where I exercise for an hour 4-5 days a week. I'm down 62 pounds. No, I'm not vegan or vegetarian, but changed to better food selections for me.

6. Live With Intention. Live with Purpose, on Purpose.

The kind of intention that puts Jesus in the spotlight. Take those dreams, goals, and ambitions He's given you and go at them, wholeheartedly, with the understanding that you are doing it for His purpose and glory, not your own. Live life like it matters because it does. The choices that you make, the things that you say, your day-to-day actions *matter*. You matter. Your opinion and your voice make a difference when you walk the talk. So, live life with the understanding that you were meant to impact the world around you.

7. Speak Life.

We read in Luke's writings,

> "The good person out of the good treasure of his heart brings forth what is good; and the evil person out of the evil treasure brings forth what is evil; for his mouth speaks from that which fills his heart."
> *Luke 6:45*

That's a fancy way of saying how we speak matters. This principle rings true whether we are speaking to others or speaking to ourselves. One sure-fire way to love yourself in a godly manner is to speak life-giving words over yourself. When I say life-giving words, I don't mean flattering affirmations (another deception of the modern self-care movement). The only effective way to speak life-giving words is to speak in agreement with the truth of the Bible. Anything less will lead you astray. When we model speaking biblical truth and life over ourselves, we teach others how to claim and believe the same biblical truth for themselves.

8. Pursue Joy.

The Bible tells us that the joy of the Lord is our strength (see Nehemiah 8:10 and Psalm 27). More often than not, when we feel exhausted and overwhelmed, it's because we've been leaning on our own strength instead of leaning into God's. Instead of giving in to temptation and following the world's principles of self-care, what we really need is to press into God and let His joy restore and strengthen us. When you give God permission to fill you up, what you'll likely discover is that what you thought was discontentment with your life or circumstances was really a hunger or thirst that cannot be quenched by anything but the joy of the Lord.

- People or relationships won't fill it.
- Hobbies won't fill it.
- Recognition won't fill it.
- Wealth won't fill it.
- **Only Jesus.**

9. Love Yourself Where You Are Now.

Don't wait. You don't have to accomplish anything spectacular to become someone worth loving. Love yourself right now right where you are.

Start with this simple prayer:

God, teach me to love myself. Teach me to view myself the same way You do so I can learn to love others with the same love you have for me. Amen.

If you're struggling to love yourself where you're at, use these Bible verses about acceptance to help you peacefully give and *receive* God's love.

> "For God so loved the world, that He gave His only Son, so that everyone who believes in Him will not perish, but have eternal life."
>
> *John 3:16*

> "But God demonstrates His own love toward us, in that while we were still sinners, Christ died for us."
>
> *Romans 5:8*

> "And let's consider how to [a]encourage one another in love and good deeds, 25 not abandoning our own meeting together, as is the habit of some people, but encouraging one another; and all the more as you see the day drawing near."
>
> *Hebrews 10:24–25*

You don't have to have it all together or have all the answers to receive God's love right here, right now.

> "Now accept the one who is weak in faith, but not to have quarrels over opinions."
>
> *Romans 14:1*

In Conclusion

I believe as we develop a proper love for God and ourselves, it will extend to the "others" in our lives: family, friends, coworkers, church, community, challenging relationships, etc. We will love according to the word of God and not our feelings or how the world says we should love.

What is Love?

My Pastor, Tony Evans, says love is "to responsibly and righteously seek the wellbeing of another."

The Bible says in 1 Corinthians 13:4–8,

> "Love is patient, love is kind, it is not jealous; love does not brag, it is not arrogant. It does not act disgracefully, it does not seek its own benefit; it is not provoked, does not keep an account of a wrong suffered, it does not rejoice in unrighteousness, but rejoices with the truth; it keeps every confidence, it believes all things, hopes all things, endures all things. Love never fails; but if there are gifts of prophecy, they will be done away with; if there are tongues, they will cease; if there is knowledge, it will be done away with."

Also, in Ephesians 4:15–16,

> "But speaking the truth in love, we are to grow up in all aspects into Him who is the head, that is, Christ, from whom the whole body, being fitted and held together by what every joint supplies, according to the proper working of each individual part, causes the growth of the body for the building up of itself in love."

ABOUT
Chaplain Dena Crecy

Dena Crecy is a believer and follower of Jesus Christ, a mother and granny, along with an author, speaker, coach, and Distinguished Toastmaster (twice). Dena loves sharing God's word. She has a unique way of connecting with her audience. She incorporates her own story as part of her authentic approach. Revelation 12:11 says, "And they have defeated him by the blood of the Lamb and by their testimony. And they did not love their lives so much that they were afraid to die."

Dena uses speaking and writing as a way to share the message of purpose God has given her. She has published two books and is a contributing author in three books. Her passion is to disciple women of God into the purposes of God in the four main areas of life—Relationships, Career, Finances, and Life Purpose—using biblical principles. This passion sparked her to form Relationships God Style, a 501c-nonprofit organization. Dena is a graduate of Grace International Seminary with a master's degree in theological studies. She is also a licensed and ordained minister of the gospel, Board Certified Mental Health Coach, and Licensed/Ordained Chaplin with Chaplains International.

Dena is a proud mother of two adult children, Andre' "Sean" Crecy and Sydney Paulette Crecy, and the blessed granny of Jaden, Kayson and Penelope.

You can reach Dena by:

- Email: relationshipsgodsyle@yahoo.com
- Phone: 469-730-4618
- Through her website: www.rgscoachingcenter.org.

> "As each one has received a special gift, employ it in serving one another as good stewards of the multifaceted grace of God."
>
> *1 Peter 4:10*

Sharing Personal Stories and Lessons Learned About Love

God, Self, Others

Ethel Marie Curtis

Love for God

> "Before I formed you in the womb I knew you, and before you were born I consecrated you; I have appointed you as a prophet to the nations."
>
> *Jeremiah 1:5*

As I reflect on this scripture, it makes me feel so good to know that even before I was in my mother's womb, my heavenly father had a plan for my life! How awesome is that? This not only applies to me, but to all mankind. We were created for God (Colossians 1:16). In God's gracious nature, He allows us to choose. So, my question to all of those who are reading this book, will you choose to make Jesus Christ Lord and Savior of your life?

I grew up in the church. My mom introduced us to Christ at a very young age. She was a preacher's kid (PK), so she made sure we knew about him. After the untimely death of my father, my mother uprooted us from West Los Angeles and relocated us to the Central Valley. My grandfather built two churches in Tulare, California: one in a place called Goshen, the other in Matheny tracks. He ministered to a small group of families who lived out in the country and to all of the local children and their families. Ministry was one of his greatest joys. He did it effortlessly. Of course, being the child of a preacher's kid, my siblings and I were required to attend church... *all of the time.* Regular service, Bible study, prayer meetings, missionary meetings, and whenever my grandfather received an invitation to preach at another church. For me, church was a chore and a weekly dread. As a child, I remember my grandparents and my mother often telling me that they'd pray every day that one day all of their children and grandchildren would get up and go to church on their own without being told. Not only that, but that they would fall in love with Jesus and have a strong relationship with him. I am happy to say that they lived to see it happen before they went on to glory (Proverbs 11:21).

I remember like it was yesterday... undergrad... party... alcoholic beverage in my hand, profanity coming out of my mouth. I remember the smirks on my friends' faces from trying to hold their laughs in before they let loose laughing hysterically. "You don't even sound right cursing! You're like a square with rounded corners!" Don't get me wrong. I'm not saying you have to be a square to live a Christian life—that's not the case. Living for Christ is an unexplainable blessing. I knew what my friends were trying to tell me, even though they may not have spoken the proper words. I knew that the Holy Spirit was tugging on my heart strings, drawing me to him. My grandparents' and mother's prayers were not in vain. Although I had given my life to Christ as a teenager, I wasn't really living for him. I'm grateful for his grace and mercy. At that time in my life, I knew him as my savior, but I hadn't let him become Lord over my life just yet. That night at that party was an eye opener for me. Slowly, the Lord began to draw me as I prayed more, studied his word more, and trusted in him more. As I learned about him on a daily basis, he taught me about myself as well. The good, bad, and ugly. A good friend of mine tells me often to trust the process. So, I'm telling you to trust the process (Philippians 1:6). Our heavenly father loves us. When he is the Lord and Savior over our lives, he's shaping and molding us into the best that we can become (Isaiah 64:8). Will you fall in love with him? Will you let him be Lord and Savior over your life?

Love for Self

> "For You created my innermost parts; You wove me in my mother's womb. I will give thanks to You, because I am awesomely and wonderfully made; Wonderful are Your works, And my soul knows it very well."
>
> *Psalm 139:13–14*

To know how special we are to God is such an amazing feeling! When I think about Love for Self, it can be demonstrated in various ways. We should all make sure that we take care of our mental, social, and physical wellbeing. I'd like to focus on showing love for ourselves by walking in forgiveness and abstaining from fornication. These are ways of honoring God in our bodies.

There was once a time in my life when I held on to unforgiveness. My unforgiveness stemmed from built up hurts throughout my life that I never really addressed. A few life experiences occurred where the Holy Spirit showed me what I needed to let go. I refused to listen to what God was trying to show me. I truly suffered the consequences. When I finally chose to forgive, I had an inner peace that I can't even explain. One thing that I know for sure is that forgiveness helps the person that has chosen to forgive. The person or people that have caused us to live in unforgiveness may not even know that they've done something wrong, or even hurt or upset us . . . and some may not even care. Whatever the case may be, guess what? They continue to live their lives while we're stuck, stagnant, and angry.

Your life will be like a hamster in a wheel. Continuous spinning, but going nowhere. We may even go through a time in our life when we think those feelings have subsided—an "Out of Sight, Out of Mind" moment—but if the unforgiveness hasn't been dealt with, it will only re-surface again and again. God loves us so much that he reveals things about ourselves to help us, not to hurt us. When he does, we need to let it go, give it to him, and he will do the rest. You may not even feel anything at first. Know this, God is working it out! You will truly know when forgiveness has taken place. Unforgiveness can affect a person physically, mentally, and spiritually.

Let it go. You don't want to experience the things that I dealt with. I had many restless, sometimes sleepless nights, and thoughts of revenge. Forgive . . . Forgive for you. Then go forth! God will complete the work that he started in you (Philippians 1:6).

So, as you continue to go forth in your new freedom, what about romantic relationships? Whether you are in a married, divorced, widowed, or single season of your life, I think we have all had thoughts about the day when we would meet our purpose partner. When we do meet that special someone, how do we conduct ourselves while dating?

From my own personal experience, I know that the Lord wants us to glorify him in our bodies. We are not our own. We were bought with a price (1 Corinthians 6:19–20).

When I re-dedicated my life to Christ, I made a vow to never defile my body again through sexual intercourse. I've been living a life of celibacy until marriage—if that's His will for my life. One thing I know for sure: HE can keep you if you want to be kept. Prayer is key! The Holy Spirit will guide your decisions. If you truly want to know if someone is worth your time, HE will reveal all things... even those red flags that we sometimes CHOOSE to ignore. Listen to His still, small voice.

There's a verse in Maverick City's song "Wait On You" that says this: "I've never seen a pot of gold at the end of the rainbow, but I've got a promise I can hold. In the middle of struggle, God if you said it, you'll perform it. May not be how I want you to, but here's what I'll do... I'm gonna wait on you!"

Whether He says yes, no, or not now, accept His answer. He knows what's best for you (Jeremiah 29:11). Surround yourself with Godly mentors, seek counseling, and make sure that your circle of friends are giving you wise advice about dating. (Ecclesiastes 4:9–12). Also, make sure that the person you're dating is honoring God in their body, too. They shouldn't be having sexual relations with someone else just because they're not having sex with you. I can't say this enough: prayer is key (1 Thessalonians 5:16–17)! Will you have your moments? Yes, you will. Remember, God's word says we have a way of escape (1 Corinthians 10:13). Along with scripture, be aware of your weaknesses, triggers, and avoid places that will cause you to fall into temptation.

If you fall, guess what? Jesus Christ gives Grace upon Grace (John 1:16). Lift your head up, and start again today! Know your worth. Love yourself.

Love for Others

When I think about Love for Others, I think about how females interact with one another. The original *Mean Girls* movie comes to my mind. This movie was released on April 30, 2004. It deals with various high school cliques and how teens can bully one another. The ultimate goal for these teens was to reach a high social status or "the in-crowd." This film grossed roughly 130.1 million dollars. Being an educator, even though this movie was very comical, it had a lot of teachable moments in it. It touches on the damaging effects that bullying and social cliques can have on teenagers. I think that the messages from this movie can be applied to adults as well. Sometimes, mean children grow up to be mean adults. It's a sad thing to say, but it's true.

It was May of 1998 when I graduated from college. I completed my undergraduate studies at Texas Southern University in Houston, Texas. It was a great experience that I'll never forget. When the graduation ceremony was over, I was a bundle of emotions. Torn between staying in Texas or moving back to California. I knew deep down that it would be best to stay in Texas, and my mother and godmother felt the same way. I disagreed with them and told them that I was moving back home. So, after graduation, I moved back to my hometown in the Central Valley of California. I soon realized that my decision to move back home was not a good one.

Even when our lives take a turn that's off track, God's divine providence can get us back on track. Every life experience is a part of His divine plan for our lives. We should try our best to maximize each season of our lives.

I began working, but only with preparations for moving in mind. Some years went by, then God opened the door for me to return to Texas. After having such a great college experience, you can imagine the shock and hurt I felt when females that looked like me displayed not so kind actions towards me when I moved back to Texas. Please understand, *it's not every female* that I've experienced this type of treatment from. I'm sharing things that have happened to me in the past and things that sometimes still happen. If you take offense to what I'm sharing, maybe you should look inside yourself and ask the question, have I ever acted unkind to someone for no apparent reason? Was this person only trying to show kindness towards me?

Girl, Why Are You So Mean?!

Anyone who knows me knows that I am very bubbly. I *love* to laugh. My family raised me to treat people how I wanted to be treated. My mother was so kind. As a teenager, I remember having conversations with her. I'd question her about the way she treated people. When she felt like my conversation was getting out of line, she'd tell me to hush and remind me that we wouldn't be on this earth forever, and she was preparing for her eternal home. She lived her life demonstrating kindness to everyone she came in contact with. The way she lived her life amazed me.

I don't want you to get confused. Salvation is a gift from God (Ephesians 2:8–10). It is by faith in Jesus Christ. Your works don't get you into heaven, but your good works on earth will increase your rewards when you stand before our heavenly father on that great day (Romans 14:10–12). The way my mom lived her life has stuck with me. One of my favorite quotes that reminds me of how my mother lived her life is by Maya Angelou: "My wish for you is that you continue. Continue to be who and how you are, to astonish a mean world with your acts of kindness."

Whether I know someone or not, if we cross paths walking down the street, at a social gathering, sporting event, church fellowship, etc. I will make eye contact, say hello, or smile. I don't have the gift of gab, but I know how to make someone feel welcome. Some ladies will return my greetings, and then there are the ones that will look at me like I'm crazy, and some will look straight through me, scowl, and act like I'm talking to the air. Have you ever been at an event where you don't know too many people, but you make it your business to introduce yourself to others? So, you walk up to a table and greet the four other females that are seated. One gives you the side eye, one scowls at you, and the other one reluctantly speaks after you ask if you can sit at their table. They say yes, but whew! The tension (of an unwanted stranger) is thick! So, after about ten uncomfortable minutes and whispers amongst these ladies, they all get up in a ripple and make their way to another table. You're left alone. . . but no worries. The table soon fills up with people who don't mind meeting new people.

Girl, Why Are You So Mean?!

On your job, have you treated another female the same way? You ignore them, roll your eyes at them, scowl at them, or turn your nose up at them when they are simply trying to be kind or make conversation with you. Have you made assumptions about them before you have personally even gotten to know them? If you hear others complimenting them, does it increase your dislike of this person even more? (Even though you have rejected all opportunities of getting to know them?) Ladies, it doesn't hurt to compliment one another.

Girl, Why Are You So Mean?!

Church girls! Are you guilty of treating other females in this way too?! I can remember being at a church event. All it took was one more time . . . one more eye roll and scowl. I thought I was strong, I thought that all of the treatment that I had experienced over the years hadn't affected me. It did. All of a sudden, tears began to uncontrollably roll down my face. I tried to stop them, but I couldn't. Soon, other females began to surround me with hugs. They thought I was being consumed by the Holy Spirit. No sister, not this time. I was tired. Tired of the treatment that I had received by so many females over the years that look... like... me.

Girl, Why Are You So Mean?!

So, you might be thinking, *I wasn't raised like she was; she doesn't know what I've been through.* You're right, I don't. I'm simply sharing what I have experienced over the years. Let me ask you this: don't you think it takes so much more energy to be mean than kind? Being mean is so much more draining. There's a quote that I often see on social media that goes like this: "Don't let someone dim your light simply because it's shining in their eyes."

Are females still acting in the way that I described above? Yes, they are. Does it bother me? Not like it used to. I recover very quickly and I count it all joy (James 1:2–4)! *I refuse to dim my light.*

Girl, Why Are You So Mean?!

> "So then, while we have opportunity, let's do good to all people, and especially to those who are of the household of the faith."
>
> *Galatians 6:10*

ABOUT

Ethel Marie Curtis

Ethel Curtis serves as a Deaconess at Oak Cliff Bible Fellowship Church in Dallas, Texas. She also serves with the Prayer ministry, Reconciliation team, and Comfort and Care. She has worked for several years in Public Service. Ethel currently works for the Dallas County Juvenile Justice Department. Ethel specializes in "Starfish Stories." Making one difference at a time. She has a B.S. in Health Education from Texas Southern University in Houston, Texas and a M.ED. in Curriculum and Instruction from Grand Canyon University in Phoenix, Arizona. Ethel is a lifetime member of the

Texas Southern University National Alumni Association and a member of Alpha Kappa Alpha Sorority, Inc.

When her schedule allows, Ethel volunteers with the Dallas Council on Alcohol and Drug Abuse. During her reign as Ms. Dallas and Ms. Texas United America in 2011-12, she focused on educating students about the harmful effects of alcohol and drugs.

Ethel enjoys spending time with her family and friends, walks on beaches, theater arts, serving in her church and local communities, and all things pageantry.

You can find her on Instagram @ethelmariecurtis or by email at shinebrightemc@yahoo.com.

> "My wish for you is that you continue. Continue to be who and how you are, to astonish a mean world with your acts of kindness."
>
> *Maya Angelou*

Soulful Embrace

Nurturing God's Gift of Self-Love

Jeannette Dixon

I rediscovered the significance of unconditional love for myself many years ago while experiencing rejection from a covenant relationship. A covenant marriage relationship is one governed by God's commands for God's glory. God's glory is on display when both the husband and the wife are faithful to those commands.

You're invited to explore further details about what I thought was a covenant committed marriage of 18 years in a previous book co-authored by me and others, titled, *Therefore, Forgive, Love, and Rest.* Perhaps your current struggle mirrors mine. Keep in mind that genuine commitment to others is only possible through wholehearted surrender and commitment to Christ. Without complete submission to Christ, there can't be a real commitment to anyone else. In the book *Therefore, Forgive, Love, and Rest,* I candidly shared some of my feeling and struggles of abandonment. Since then, God has continued to protect me, sustain me, promote me, and nurture me. The lyrics from Richard Smallwood's song "Trust Me" is a reminder that God was and is with me. Others may walk away, but God will never leave me. God is close to the brokenhearted and He rescues those whose spirits are crushed (Psalms 34:18–19). God assures us of deliverance when we place our trust in Him. During that challenging season, it became very crucial for me to be reminded by God Himself that I was and I am valuable and precious to Him, and so are you.

I considered it imperative to explore the definition for self-love as I began on the journey of rediscovering what self-love is and what self-love is not. As I began my journey, I observed that the trauma of rejection had caused God's truth about my identity to become obscured, thus making it difficult for me to understand the value of appreciating and loving myself. I could no longer trust my blurred vision for the truth; instead, I had to turn back to God's word to regain clarity.

As we delve into our identity in Christ and discover ways to reestablish a connection with self-love, we will use the following questions as a guide: Do you love yourself? How do you know that you love yourself? What actions are you taking to validate your love for yourself?

Definition of Self-Love

Biblical self-love must first begin with loving God. Matthew 22:37–38 states, "And He said to him, 'You shall love the Lord your God with all your heart, and with all your soul, and with all your mind.' This is the great and foremost commandment." This is the first and greatest commandment. It sets the foundation that makes it possible for us to love others and ourselves in the proper context.

Following God's first commandment creates an environment that makes it possible for us to love others and to cultivate a wholesome and healthy love for ourselves. The self-love that we talk about throughout this chapter is one that is wholesome, selfless, and unconditional. It is a love that is guarded and grounded in our identity in Christ Jesus.

In 1 Corinthians 13, God paints a vivid picture of what love is and what love is not. This canvas covers all forms and expressions of love, even our self-love.

God said, "Love is patient, love is kind, it is not jealous; love does not brag, it is not arrogant. It does not act disgracefully, it does not seek its own benefit; it is not provoked, does not keep an account of a wrong suffered."

Perhaps, the above verse is prompting you to reflect on a situation or on someone who claimed to love you. Now, you can clearly see the shortcomings of that love based on God's definition of love. It may be an opportunity for us to examine our own hearts and motives assessing whether we have practiced the fruits of love as defined by God, even towards ourselves. Do we find that it's easier to display patience, kindness, and love toward everyone else but ourselves? Do we find that forgiving others comes easier than forgiving ourselves?

We can bridge the biblical concepts above with those of Jeffrey Borenstein, President of the Brain and Behavior Research Foundation, who defines love for one's self as a state of appreciation for oneself that grows from actions that support our physical, psychological and spiritual growth.

Question to Ponder: Do I love myself and if I do, how do I recognize that I do?

Defined by Christ

Let's start with the WO-man in the mirror and rediscover—or perhaps discover for the first time—what God says. God says I am *valuable*, I am *precious*, and I am His *righteousness* because Christ died on the cross for me.

The mere essence of being defined by Christ is to *know* who or what does not have the ability to define me, including circumstances, seasons, rejection, or the culture. Being a productive citizen and a servant of God are commendable qualities, but they are not the totality of who God says that I am. My Pastor reminds us of how valuable we are to God through the following example: "A crisp and clean $100 bill that is crumbled up, thrown to the ground, stepped on, and rubbed in the dirt still maintains its value." Just like that $100 bill, whether it's crisp or crumpled up, I am purposefully valuable to God. Each note of a $100 bill has a different serial number. Just like each bill is unique, so are each of us. There are over 8 billion people in the world, yet David reminds us in Psalms 139 that, "I am fearfully and wonderfully made." We are so valuable to God that He crafted each of us with immense care and attention. We are so loved by God that He created us uniquely different from each of those billions of people in the world. I can boast in the truth stated by Isaiah 64:8: "Yet you, LORD, are our Father. We are the clay, you are the potter; we are all the work of your hand."

Balancing Act of Self-Love

My self-love journey has often seemed like the teeter-totter game that I played on as a child. A teeter-totter, often referred to as a seesaw, is a long narrow board with a center point. Usually, one side of the board is up high in the air while the other side is down low on the ground. Learning to love myself has often seemed like that kind of experience. When circumstances in life were going well, it seemed effortless to love myself unconditionally. When my health was good, when a relationship was budding, and when my finances were balanced, that tetter-totter feeling is breathtaking! The consuming feeling is like a fluttering wind brushing across my face, forcing me to laugh and scream out the words, "LOOK AT ME!" Oh, what a feeling! I love me some me when all is going well.

> "Life is like a seesaw, sometimes you are up and sometimes you are down. How you handle the ups and downs is about you, not the seesaw."
>
> *Sue DeCacco*

But hold on—inevitably, circumstances or seasons in life change, and when that happens, often I can be consumed with a myriad of questions, more questions than I have answers for. I have discovered that I must be careful and intentional about believing who I am and whose I am, especially when I am feeling rejected, unloved, or the promotion didn't happen— the list can go on and on. These uncomfortable seasons and circumstances can cause me to quickly foster a negative relationship with myself. That negative self-relationship can cause doubt and disbelief that are contrary to the word of God. In fact, the creeping thoughts can cause us to question our worth, undermining the truth of our inherent value as declared by God. Isaiah 53:1 challenges us with the following question: "Who has believed our report?" *And to whom has the arm of the Lord been revealed?*

We live in a world that's inundated with reports that want to define who we are. We can get reports from the news media, social media, podcast, apps, websites, search engines, and Satan's reports all attempting to define us.

But then there is God's report. God's report says I am healed (Jeremiah 17:14) and I am loved (John 15:9).

Question to Ponder: Whose report will you believe?

As a Christian, I know that self-love and self-care must first begin with God's truth about me so that I can rightly claim my identity. Self-love is about being patient and kind to myself, even when I make a mistake. Self-love is essential to fulfilling the commandment in Matthew 22:39: *"Love your neighbor* as *yourself."*

God's truth says that I am valuable because of what I cost. As one loved by God, I have also been chosen by God for "adoption as sons through Jesus Christ to Himself" (Ephesians 1:4–5). Yet, on occasion, we are challenged with believing the truth. God says I am more precious than jewels and my worth is far above rubies or pearls. I must choose to believe God's truth.

Satan is cunning and he is a deceiver. He can deceive us by enticing us to participate in negative self-talk reinforcing the belief that I am not valuable. When self-doubt creeps in, I must always turn those negative thoughts and negative self-talk into positive thoughts and positive self-talk to remind myself of who I am in Christ.

God's Affirmations

Begin the process by confronting every negative thought with a positive affirmation. Acknowledge and talk about your strengths that God has gifted you. Reaffirm your identity based on how God defines you. The pivot from negative self-talk to positive self-talk may not happen overnight, but with perseverance and the help of the Holy Spirit, you can and you will cultivate a new Godly-growth mindset.

Another challenge that can threaten our truth of who God says I am is rejection. Rejection in simple terms is when we feel pushed away or unwanted. The pushed-away or unwanted feelings could be the results of an unwanted divorce, a long-term relationship that didn't turn out the way you hoped it would, the promotion you didn't get, on and on.

In a teeter-totter or seesaw game, balance is crucial. Similarly, the goal of self-love involves finding equilibrium between self-love and external factors. Be careful that external factors don't overpower the truth of who you are and negatively affect your self-worth, thus affecting your self-love. Too much focus on one side may result in an imbalance, compromising the truth of God.

Initiating Self-Love

Understanding the essence of self-love marks the starting point for mastering its mechanics. It incorporates the act of self-compassion, forgiveness, patience, kindness, and acceptance. It is an awareness of our own worth and determination to not only prioritize self-love, but to also protect it. Loving ourselves involves actively taking steps to nurture and to care for one's well-being. Biblical scriptures remind us that, above all else, guard your heart for it is the wellspring of life. This scripture is saying that above all else, we must guard ourselves. We must guard, nourish, and care for our heart because it matters to Him (Proverbs 4:23).

Mirror Practice Affirmations

Practicing self-love affirmations in front of a mirror is a powerful way to cultivate a positive and nurturing relationship with oneself based on the word of God. Here are some ideas for incorporating mirror practice using biblical self-love affirmations.

Replace Your Words with God's Words

- Point to yourself in the mirror and repeat that I am loved just as I am (Ephesians 2:8).
- I will *give thanks* and praise to *You*, for I am fearfully and *wonderfully* made; *Wonderful* are *Your*

works, and my soul *knows* it *very well (Psalm 139:14)*.

- I am strong and courageous (Joshua 1:9).
- I am chosen, I am royalty (1 Peter 2:9).
- I am forgiven (Matthew 6:14–15).
- I am the daughter of a King (Psalm 45:9).

Mirror Story

In a fictional narrative, the author tells a story about a young lady who lived in a quiet village whose name was Emma. Emma was known for her kindness and generosity, always putting others before herself. She had a heart of gold but often forgot to extend the same warmth to herself.

One day, as Emma strolled through the village square, she noticed an old, dusty mirror in the corner of a small antique shop. The shopkeeper explained that the mirror had a unique quality—it reflected not just physical appearances but also the true feelings within.

Intrigued, Emma decided to purchase the mirror. As she gazed into it for the first time, she saw not only her reflection but also the exhaustion in her eyes, the weight on her shoulders from constantly catering to the needs of others.

Determined to change this, Emma began a daily ritual. Every morning, she stood in front of the mirror and spoke words of affirmation to herself. "I am worthy of love. I deserve happiness. I am enough just as I am."

As days turned into weeks, something magical happened. Emma's reflection began to change. The weariness in her eyes transformed into a sparkle of self-assurance, and the heaviness on her shoulders lifted. The village noticed the change in Emma—she walked with a newfound confidence, and her generosity now stemmed from a place of self-love rather than obligation.

One afternoon, Emma came across a young girl sitting alone by the village fountain, looking dejected. Instead of immediately offering assistance, Emma paused, looked into the mirror she always carried, and reminded herself of her own worth. With a heart filled with self-love, she approached the girl, offering not just help but genuine compassion.

Word of Emma's transformation spread through the village, inspiring others to embrace self-love. The dusty mirror became a symbol of empowerment, as villagers began to recognize the importance of caring for oneself in order to authentically care for others.

And so, in that little village, a simple mirror became a catalyst for a powerful lesson—that true kindness and love begin with oneself. Emma's journey of self-love not only changed her life but also radiated outward, leaving an indelible mark on the hearts of those she touched.

Similar to Emma, we have the opportunity to adopt a daily ritual. Stand before the mirror each day and affirm positive words to yourself. Embrace and believe in the power of those affirmations. Believe the words of affirmation that you speak.

God's inerrant and infallible words remind me that:
- I am a child of God
- I am never alone
- I am a new creation
- I am chosen
- I am accepted
- I am forgiven
- I am loved
- I am His beloved
- I am fearfully and wonderfully made

Like Emma, we can begin walking with a newfound confidence grounded in the flawless word of God because of who we are and who we belong to.

Questions to Ponder

Do I notice a pivot in my mindset?

How can I use this catalyst to encourage and to inspire myself and others?

Deceptive Lies: Divine Truth

John 10:10 reminds us, "The thief comes only to steal and kill and destroy; I came so that they would have life, and have it abundantly." *Be on Guard.* As we work to develop a Godly mindset regarding our value and self-worth, the enemy is persistently trailing us trying to snatch away God's truth for his deceptive lies. The enemy often tries to convince us that we are undeserving of love—even our own self-love. Whether you have been disappointed by someone, deeply hurt by a trusted individual, wounded deeply by a loved one, or perhaps you have prayed for years without seeing the manifestation of those prayers, dear sisters, understand that as long as you have breath in your lungs, God continues to work marvelously and miraculously within you and through you, despite any temporary setbacks to your self-worth caused by others' words or actions or your own.

Question to Ponder

What will you do to embrace God's divine truth?

My Role: Believe

Believing that I am valuable and precious begins with a mindset that chooses to *know* that Jesus loved me so much that He died for me. God has always and will always love me. I am His precious chosen daughter. God's love is eternal. Psalm 100:5 says, "The LORD is good; His mercy is everlasting and His faithfulness is to all generations."

Reconciliation

If you need restoration, begin with your relationship with God. Ask God's forgiveness for any sin that you may have overtly or covertly committed. Paul declares in Romans 5:10, "For if while we were enemies we were reconciled to God through the death of His Son, much more, having been reconciled, we shall be saved by His life." This is the only way a person can be reconciled to God. Then ask God to teach you to forgive yourself and to forgive others so that you can be reconciled with others. "Therefore, if you are presenting your offering at the altar, and there you remember that your brother has something against you, leave your offering there before the altar and go; first be reconciled to your brother, and then come and present your offering." (Matthew 5:23–24).

Encourage and Inspire Others

My Pastor often emphasizes to us that when God blesses us, we should practice being a conduit rather than a cul-de-sac. A cul-de-sac is stuck in one place, confined to a dead-end street. It is not connected to another road or anything else. On the other hand, a conduit allows God's power to flow through us to benefit others. God's purpose is to bless the world with the blessings of Abraham. God wants us to be a conduit, not a cul-de-sac, of God's blessing. Genesis 12:2–3 says, "I will make you into a great nation, and I will bless you, and make your name great, and you shall be a blessing; and I will bless those who bless you, and the one who curses you I will curse; and in you all the families of the earth will be blessed."

Know that you are unconditionally loved by God, Embrace your self-love as a gift from God. Dear sisters and brothers, know that you are precious in God's eyes, you have value, and you are significant to God. Know that as long as breath is in your lungs, despite what someone did or said to you that may have temporarily diminished your self-worth, God continues to work marvelously and miraculously in you and through you.

God's inerrant and infallible Word Says, "When you pass through the waters, I will be with you; and through the rivers, they will not overflow you. When you walk through the fire, you will not be scorched, nor will the flame burn you" (Isaiah 43:2). God, *not* the enemy, has the right to define you because He created you in *His* image. Embrace His truth and practice loving God, yourself, and others according to God's command. Your identity is shaped by His hands and *not* the whispers of a deceitful enemy.

ABOUT

Jeannette Dixon

Jeannette Dixon wears several hats with pride and purpose. Jeannette is proud to be a mother, Mimi, author, and a devoted leader at Oak Cliff Bible Fellowship Church. Within the Women of Transformation Ministry, Jeannette leads as a Devotional and Prayer leader, committed to guiding women towards spiritual healing and victory in Christ. She is a co-founder of Godly Marriage Readiness.

Jeannette has attained her Bachelor's Degree from the University of Southern Mississippi, Master's Degree from Sarasota University, and pursued Educational Leadership classes through the McNeil Foundation.

Deeply rooted in her faith, Jeannette is dedicated to delving into scriptures and embodying the essence of a Kingdom Woman.

Jeremiah affirms that God is in control and moreover, He has good things in store.

> "'For I know the plans that I have for you,' declares the Lord, 'plans for prosperity and not for disaster, to give you a future and a hope.'"
>
> *Jeremiah 29:11*

The Journey of Self-Discovery

Dr. Delores McLaughlin

What if you had six months to live—how would you value that time? Even though we probably have longer to live, ask yourself, *What love messages am I sharing with others on a daily basis?* Agape love is an unconditional connection that exceeds merely loving others and understanding them, but a love that breaks through the deeper approach of loving others when you don't understand.

John 3:16 says, "For God so loved the world, that He

gave His only Son, so that everyone who believes in Him will not perish, but have eternal life." The love of God is unconditional, needing nothing in return. Where is your love positioned? Do you expect something in return when you give, share, or make a sacrifice?

Agape love is sacrificial when you surrender yourself to be obedient to our Lord and Savior Jesus Christ. Understanding is important, but sometimes you are ordered to do things that you don't understand, to have faith and trust in Jesus Christ. Reflecting over the past year, I didn't understand what God was teaching me about agape love until I came face to face with church members who persecuted, lied, and slandered my name, reputation, and everything of value to me. These were the members I needed to forgive and surrender unconditional love. But deep in my heart, I screamed out, "No way!" I wouldn't surrender to what I felt in my heart. But it was God's way of getting me to let go of the past and understanding how love works when you are trusting God.

Love is not understanding why you do what you do but knowing love is the key factor in doing everything you do. Love is substantial in living life based on relationships and doing the right things for the right reasons regardless of the outcome. Our first relationship is the one with Jesus Christ, and then all other relationships follow His relationship. Being brought up in a Christian home with my siblings, we were taught how to follow the commandments of God by being responsible for the decisions made in our lives. I never doubted true love or questioned it. Life without love can be a miserable one.

I was in a marriage in my early 20s that centered more on convenience than love. This mindset encouraged me to sit around, crying with tears rolling down my face, holding my head down with a low self-esteem. One way out of any struggle in life is to hold on to God regardless of what other folks say, do, or how you are treated. I divorced this man after five years of marriage. Having love that moves you is the joy and peace which encourages a life of love by living on purpose.

Love has changed me in a way I never expected. It was by the grace of God that I began to understand the assignment that I had been given by God. I trusted the assignment and began to say, "I am good enough because I was chosen by the King himself." I imagined myself sitting next to the King and receiving the love that was needed in my life. I started to feel that my journey of discovery had nothing to do with others but everything to do with me and my agape love, including my stance on accepting and forgiving others. Then, my journey transformed into awareness of my love, passion, and self-discovery.

I chose to participate in this project because of the lack of love that is displayed as authentic love. How does one know what to believe as truth when confusion seems to follow every step? The love of importance is giving others what they need with no expectations. After experiencing my journey involving my mother's illness, it allowed me to truly understand that some people have conditions on the love they share. If you are capable of giving the person what is needed from you, then the love continues. But when change comes—for example, an illness or death—then the love message changes. Otherwise, the love factor will change, no questions asked.

Love is on the move means "constant change." You don't know how it is going to change, but it will, and you must be ready to flow with the change regardless of the challenges and outcomes. As a vessel of love, you must be willing to persevere. Don't look for others to direct you or help out because their mission can be about other motives and they might not be willing to assist when needed. Their love could be conditional and not unconditional.

I remembered receiving a call and the person on the other end of the phone asked, "Is this Delores McLaughlin?" and I said, "Yes, it is." The man continued with a caring and calm response: "Delores, my name is Sergeant Robertson. Your mother wanted me to call you. She has been in a car accident, but she is doing okay. She has a few bruises with the airbag coming out but refuses to go to the hospital. She wanted me to call you to come and pick her up." I looked at the work I needed to complete but, shrugging my shoulders, I said, "Oh, well, I've got to take care of Mom." Love can be a battlefield if you let the battle overtake the unconditional love and respond in a way that does not prioritize what needs to happen.

My real journey started after the car accident when my mother became forgetful remembering family names. I did not understand the memory lapse. Although I was a nurse for 30-plus years, this was an elevated experience that I could not explain and refuse to ponder. My Mom was an active church pastor who held special events, which were often handled well by her. But something was not the same, especially when her gaze was pointed, lost, fearful, and her gait was uncertain or one of escape. How does one handle or accept something you cannot comprehend? Most people would say to trust God and he will handle what you can't comprehend. But living this reality with someone you love so dearly is challenging, fearful, and sometimes has many moments of not knowing how to handle this new experience.

My mother was the friend that most people dreamed about; she was stern, truthful, and had an emphasis of love in her voice. She asked the questions that a lot of people think about but never ask. She would walk up to you and say, "So, what has God called you to do?" "How long have you been in ministry?" Needless to say, she was often misunderstood but never questioned. Does this approach encapsulate the love that we so much need, or is this an excuse to only deal with those love factors that we understand?

Lack of understanding can cause the love that is said to be present in our lives to become stale and questionable. A handful of the Church leaders requested a meeting with me as I was the Vice-President of the church board, and I agreed to the meeting. We prayed and everything seem to be starting off fine. But the questions started coming and penetrating like fiery darts. The spirit of love and understanding was nowhere to be found. I questioned the leaders again regarding the purpose of the meeting. I asked, "Are we here to aid the pastor in her time of need, shower the pastor with agape love even though we don't understand the reason for the season?" As I looked around the table, I realized that this wasn't about anyone else but about what God was working in and through me. My love was going to be tested in a way I never experienced, but I knew what I needed was to "raise my eyes to the mountains; from where will my help come?" (Psalm 121:1).

The Word of God will give you the necessary strength, in knowing that only God can make things happen. The importance of maintaining love in our hearts is not allowing others' attitudes and behaviors to impact our reactions relative to whatever is going on in their lives. Walking in the spirit of God guides you when reaching a change or a peak in your life. Many people ask, how do I handle this change that I don't understand, and how will this help me move forward in loving God, self, and others? This question is substantial in getting a better understanding of love. The constant move of love was more than my heart had bargained for, but understanding the assignment was crucial. According to Romans 8:28, "And we know that God causes all things to work together for good to those who love God, to those who are called according to His purpose." Once again, the love of God's Word is a treasure which is the bread of life.

> "God is love, and the one who remains in love remains in God, and God remains in him."
>
> *1 John 4:16*

Walking in God's Word is a daily lifestyle, as is walking in God's love. Unconditional love is not something we put on and take off. You must understand the Love of God and how His love has changed your life. The understanding of love is vital to your comprehension of what God wants you to do. The best way to recognize true Christians is by their love for one another. 1 John 3:18 says, "Let's not love with word or with tongue, but in deed and truth."

What love means to me is the individual must stand in truth, love, and obedience. Relationships are built on these three factors. When two parties know the truth, love comes naturally. There is a love for God, self, each other, and a love for Jesus Christ and His Church. There are no restrictions in what God allows you to experience during this journey.

Sometimes, the Lord is positioning you for a new experience, one you never knew you could go through. After my mother's car accident, things became worse and she continued to have various episodes of syncope, falls, and eventually a fractured left hip, surgery, rehab, hospitalizations, and finally hospice care. Love was constantly on the move in my life caring for my mother, no; distance was too far and no care was too much. This was a place I'd never been, and I was praying that other family members, church members, and friends would understand how love was on the move with the urgency of fulfilling the needs of my mother, no matter what she needed.

My relationship with God changed when my mother was hospitalized. I remembered the numerous sacrifices of traveling a long distance to be with her in the morning and evening to get her ready for bed. One night after getting her ready for bed, she told me to sit down next to her. Although I was already in a chair next to the bed, she said, "No, Dee, I need you to sit here on the bed with me." As I sat next to her, Mom's eyes shifted to a deep twinkle and locked into my gaze. She began to speak: "Sister, you continue to preach the true word of God and you stay put." Listening to her instructions, I began to question, *Why is she saying this to me because she is not going anywhere?* But leaving her room that night, something was different, and I realize that my mother said to me what needed to be said to continue her ministry that was built on truth, love, and obedience to Jesus Christ. Three months later, my mother transitioned/died to be with the Lord.

Love is about finding out who you are. You cannot love others without loving God first and then yourself. When I stopped focusing on how I felt and focusing on what my assignment was with my mother's well-being, my life changed. My love experiences were many, such as Agape (unconditional) and Storge (Family Love), the love experiences from that point on were a supernatural move by the Holy Spirit. This required me to surrender all in love to my mother and serve, navigating through life's challenges with everything I had, being present in love, truth, and active in obedience to God.

Three main points inspired me in my self-discovery journey:

1. Love and stay on purpose. God allowed you to be where you are for a specific reason and season.
2. You can't rush and resonate unconditional love. Enjoy the journey that the Lord has established for you, loving God, self, and others in excellence!
3. Don't allow fear to hold you back from loving unconditionally.

I feel blessed and highly favored for embracing the love of Jesus Christ daily. I am not enslaved to evil, sin, or negativity but liberated and free in sharing the love of Christ!

ABOUT

Dr. Delores McLaughlin

Dr. Delores Ramsey McLaughlin is a motivational speaker who can inspire audiences from corporate to faith based. She has a gift of making the most serious topics become less intimidating and more accepting. Delores is the founder and executive director of All Out Communication and Freedom-N-Christ Global Outreach Ministries. Delores teaches effective communication and leadership skills, strategies to successfully pursue your dreams, and how to bridge gaps between cultural and religious differences. Delores' passions lie in communicating on all levels to maintain effective communication. Dr. Delores is the Pastor of Holy Ghost Filled Church of Miracles in Phoenix, Arizona. She also enjoys being an educator, nurse, communication coach, and author.

Contact Information:

Post Box 8205

Phoenix, Arizona 85066

nthaeyezz@cox.net

> For God has not given us a spirit of timidity, but of power and love and discipline.
>
> *2 Timothy 1:7*

Love is Vitamin C for the Soul

Dr. Willene Seaverson

L ove is the soul's Vitamin C. Being loved and showing love to others is vital for a fulfilling life, much as Vitamin C is for health. Whereas Vitamin C is required for the formation and maintenance of bodily tissues and cells, love is required for the healing of trauma and any wounds received along the path of life. Love is the foundation for meaningful relationships and emotional well-being. Similarly, the people we surround ourselves with can provide a firm foundation on which to build a "house of love" or a "love shack."

For me, participating in this project was a spiritual healing experience. I was looking for answers to my long-held questions about love. I asked God to show me how to better love those around me and myself. I needed help to forgive those who did not treat me with the respect I deserved. Sometimes, that meant forgiving myself for failing to treat myself with the respect I deserved. I wanted to share my story regarding some of my love experiences since, according to Revelations 12:11, we conquer Satan by the blood of the Lamb and the word of our testimony. The simplest testimony that we all share is that I was born. I was shaped by sin. I needed a Savior. He loved me so much that He laid down His life for me to wash away my sins. Once I have confessed with my mouth and believe in my heart that Jesus Christ was raised from the dead, I am saved. I now have a right to the tree of life. I will live eternally because of LOVE.

Love for God

I discovered that my life became significantly easier when I chose to love God's way. When I chose to align my love with the patterns of this world, I suffered far more emotional conflict, bumps, and bruises. The most effective way for me to learn to love is to ask the One who made me and created love. He teaches me through His Word how to love myself and others the way I was designed to love.

Love is a journey of growth and forgiveness. If God can forgive me, I can also forgive myself. Since God has lavished His love on me, I can lavish my love on others and forgive them like God can when I am wronged. To me, "love is on the move" implies that we (God's creation) are the conduits or "pipeline" that send and receive love. The entire reason we were created on this planet was to share God's love, form bonds, and make loving connections so that others might choose to accept Jesus as their personal Savior.

We are also instructed to go into the world and make disciples and baptize in the name of the Father, the Son, and the Holy Spirit (Matthew 1:19). If we do these things, it demonstrates that we have made a commitment to Jesus and decided to follow Him. We express our love for God by obeying his commands. The Word of God reminds us to prioritize seeking God's kingdom and His way of doing things (in love), and everything else will be added to us. One of my favorite scriptures (Psalm 37:4) reminds us that when we delight in the Lord, He will grant us our heart's desires.

My relationship with God has changed after my salvation experience because I no longer simply say I love others; I genuinely do. And my heart's desire is to be Jesus' hands and feet, serving others.

Love for Self

How can I demonstrate that I love myself?

One important aspect of love is self-love and self-care. Give your body the finest nutrition, environment, and opportunity. I once recognized that I was sabotaging myself since I wasn't pursuing my goals. I was playing it safe. I was worried about what others thought of me. Quite frankly, I didn't believe I was good enough, pretty enough, or intelligent enough. The truth is that none of us can ever be enough.

Throughout my journey, I have learned how to better love myself. I fuel myself with God's word. I'm getting appropriate rest. I am accountable. I'm putting myself in the best position to nurture myself, my family, and my household. I think of myself as a leader in no matter what capacity I am in. I enjoy trying new things. I keep myself linked-in. I maintain myself emotionally, financially, physically, spiritually and I keep myself mentally energized. That's what love is all about.

It is a choice to spread love. I can do whatever it takes to think exclusively about myself and make myself happy, but I've discovered that giving and serving others makes me the happiest. However, it is important to maintain some boundaries with love. One thing I've learned over the years is the importance of self-evaluation. When a situation arises, I am sensitive enough to the prompting of the Holy Spirit to apply the wisdom I have learned on the journey of love.

After years of counseling, I realized that there were numerous occasions when I engaged in self-sabotaging conduct. These actions revealed that I did not love myself as God intended. I had to make the decision to distance myself from dangerous locations, poisonous ideas, and toxic people to create a warm environment in which to grow.

My goal is to surround myself with people who will pour back into me and make me feel validated and appreciated. If individuals cannot do this for me, the only thing I can do is pray for them and love them from a distance. A friend of mine informed me about a statement she valued from Iyanla Vanzant: "You don't have to set yourself on fire to keep others warm."

The greatest approach for me to learning to love myself and others is to educate myself on healthy types of love and seek to love the way that God intended. This requires daily practice!

In 2006, I was asked whether I would be willing to be a surrogate mother for a family that was unable to have children. Their tale struck my heart since they had an unsuccessful adoption the previous year. This time, the family decided to pay a mother to bear a surrogate baby for them. I spoke with my then-husband, who was incarcerated at the time. He knew I was struggling without his income at home. We agreed that it would be a win-win for me to carry this child for this couple that I valued as family.

The problem was that before I could complete the procedure of being inseminated with the adoptive father's sperm, I discovered I was already pregnant with a child I conceived in an extramarital affair. Since my then-husband and I did not have this child together, I found myself in a very precarious situation. The child's biological father initially wanted me to seek an abortion and handle the situation differently. I felt lost.

I decided to give birth and care for the child. However, the family reassured me that they were ecstatic for the opportunity to adopt this child, care for her, and even allow me to visit her as they raised her. This setup seemed ideal at first, but after a few visits, the adoptive parents wrote me a letter saying that I could no longer visit. There was nothing I could do because we had already signed the official adoption paperwork that their lawyer had prepared, crossing every t and dotting every i that had terminated my parental rights. I honestly felt that I had lost love during this season. My children who remained saw me carry this child for nine months and were questioning what happened. One of my daughters with a similar complexion to the daughter I surrendered told me, "You gave away the only person in the family who looks like me!"

The man I was officially married to had been incarcerated for three years and was fine with me carrying a child for another family, albeit he was initially unaware of my unplanned pregnancy. Instead of telling him right away when I found out about my surprise, I waited until after I had the child and surrendered her. This added insult to injury: embarrassment, shame, and guilt. My first husband didn't realize the baby was my biological child until after she was born. When he realized the truth, he was tremendously distressed. He wanted to divorce me. I was angry and resentful of the circumstances that led to his three-year prison sentence. And he was angry and bitter over my half-truths and lies. We split and remarried, but the bitterness and animosity about this situation with the child remained, causing tension and mistrust long after I believed we had mended and remarried. Eventually, we divorced again.

You can't turn love on and off like a faucet. I love this child just like I love my other daughters, whom I raised. God can create some beautiful things from our missteps. My story of love can be best summarized with the words of Romans 8:28: "All things work together for good for those who love the Lord and are called according to His purpose."

God has loved me despite my shortcomings and negative behavior, which resulted in the birth of a child from an extramarital affair. I was looking for love in all the wrong places, and I made the mistake of trying to fill my voids with attention from someone who was not my husband.

After I placed my child for adoption, the enemy tried to convince me that I was a bad mother and undeserving of someone's love because I refused to assume responsibility for appreciating the gift that God had bestowed upon me. However, love changes your perspective. I now see that I gave this baby girl a gift that showed my love for her and the family I gave the opportunity to raise her. As of today, this daughter is 17 and an honor student at the University of Houston. She has won awards in art, coding and is brilliant. Even though I have not seen her in person or spoken to her since she was three, the Lord has sent angels to let me know she is well taken care of and is flourishing. I can't wait to have a relationship with her one day. The enemy can't kill, steal, or destroy pure love. In the meantime, I am always praying for her and rooting for her.

1 Corinthians 13:7–9 reminds me that love never fails. It bears all, endures all, and never ends. There is an interaction between love and faith. I hope that one day I will have a phenomenal relationship with this daughter and simply move forward in love.

Another lesson I have learned in self-love is that I may have to be the change I want to see in life. I continually ask God to awaken His gifts within me so that I embody the qualities of agape love.

Without God, we are nothing but filthy rags. True love means allowing God's Word to define and strengthen us. I now sincerely feel that I can do everything through Christ, who strengthens me (Philippians 4:13). I now treat others with the same kindness that I know I should have for myself. Now I understand that love looks like getting enough rest, paying attention to my body, and taking the time to truly listen to the Holy Spirit's prompts. Love is a choice about how much time and energy I want to invest in others, especially if it means depleting myself. Remember, whatever you feed will grow, and whatever you starve will die, so if a relationship is worth it, be intentional about nurturing and pouring love into it.

Love for Others

We have a stronger foundation to support us as we fly in love if we maintain healthy relationships with the positive people in our lives. For me, demonstrating love means being kind and generous to others, as well as extending the same comfort and grace that the Lord gives to us. To love others in a healthy way, you must ACT (Accept them, Be compassionate towards them, Treat them kindly).

What is love for others? Love is the ability to see past people's flaws and into their needs. Love is about being humble—the bigger person. Love is an attempt to comprehend why another behaves the way they do, practice compassion, and outdo the other in kindness, sacrificial giving, respect, and appreciation of the other person. Love is striving to see the best in the other person, even when they don't deserve it.

One key life lesson I learned is that love looks different for different people. I hesitate to admit that I have been married to three different men (including being married two different times to my first husband). They all loved me quite differently! One of the challenges I experienced with my second husband was that he tried to rule over me—manage, control, and treat me the way a father would handle his rebellious teenage daughter. I thought I'd have to divorce myself to stay married to him. Hindsight is 20/20, and I'm not proud of having only been married to my second husband for 224 days. However, I've learned that you meet a person's representative first, so be cautious. If you give love enough time, you will notice people's true colors. You must ask God for discernment and wisdom to make sure you are not painting red flags pink. It makes no difference if someone is ordained as a minister or has a phenomenal physique; you will recognize true love by the fruit growing on people's branches. Look for love, joy, peace, patience, kindness, goodness, faithfulness, and self-control in every season of life (winter, spring, summer, and fall).

Ephesians 5:1–2 reminds us: "Be imitators of God, as beloved children; and walk in love, just as Christ also loved you and gave Himself up for us, an offering and a sacrifice to God as a fragrant aroma." In 1 Corinthians 13:4–5, Paul is asking us to look at ourselves and see if we are operating in true love: "It does not act disgracefully, it does not seek its own benefit; it is not provoked, does not keep an account of a wrong suffered."

Love keeps no record of wrongs, and love lets people live (remain alive). Love is not supposed to hurt or snuff the life out of a person. Unfortunately, people are only human and may lack the ability to love at the highest level (agape). Think about your family members—parents, spouses, kids, siblings, in-laws, friends, co-workers, and even your enemies. They may not have received the same training as you have about love's lessons, or maybe their background was in "tough love" from Hard Knock University. Although patience is a fruit of the spirit, there are many times when I have flunked my own coursework in love, especially in moments plagued with misunderstandings, disagreements, or disasters. These incidents can either bring people closer together or separate them further.

Love considers what a person is going through without holding them liable for their flaws and failings. Finally, it is important to accept the individual for who they are rather than trying to alter them. Love is doing whatever it takes to have a pleasant attitude toward others and have positive interactions as much as possible.

We may need to love those who speak brutally to us, appear to knock us down, or break their commitments. You don't have to be best friends with a toxic person or put up with narcissistic behavior if it is killing you softly, but it certainly helps to be able to make a decision to forgive and move on in love.

If you pay attention, care for, and cultivate your connection, it will be easier to love. This book taught me that, in the end, grownups are like hurt young children. When adults are offended, they may be inclined to give up or not work to correct the situation.

Love is making a decision or choice that states, "No matter what, I am for you, I want the best for you, and I will keep my promise to you." Should we all challenge ourselves to treat people as Jesus would? Absolutely! How did Jesus handle others? Although he knew we would fall short, He chose to walk in love and forgiveness, despite knowing our weaknesses. He still demonstrated sympathy and empathy. Even when sentenced to death on the cross, he uttered in Luke 23:34, "Father, forgive them; for they do not know what they are doing." That's love!

How do you like to wear your hair? Make sure you don't get so lost in "love for others" that you forget about love for yourself. If a situation does not serve you or is stressing you, get out! God created you to be who you are with your unique set of likes and dislikes. Don't live for another person. Your primary concern should be to try to please God.

You cannot change anybody, so if this person already has red flags that you are painting pink, don't proceed. Just say no. Stop, drop, and roll out of the relationship before you walk down the aisle. Don't try to stop anyone from being who they are.

Final analogy: today, I ate a salad. I wanted olives, onions, feta cheese, vinegar, oil, oregano, and ground turkey in my salad. If my salad were missing a few of the ingredients, would it still be a good salad? Yes. Are there some ingredients I would like to have in my salad that I did not name? Absolutely. My husband (number three) loves cayenne pepper on everything, so the ingredients for his dream salad may be different from my preferences. However, if we give each other the freedom to select what complements our individual taste buds, we can both be happy and eat a salad we love. All in all, love is the spice of life. Some people (like family) we cannot choose, but we were born unto. With others, we can make a decision if the relationship is for a reason, a season, or a lifetime. No matter what you encounter on this journey of love, remember to take your Vitamin C.

You need Vitamin C to repair your tissues and heal your body. Don't forget to take Jesus, too. He is the best restorer and healer I know.

If you have had a few bumps and bruises along this love journey, don't worry. Philippians 4:8 reminds us to think about whatever things are true, honorable, right, pure, lovely, and of good repute. If there is any excellence and if anything is worthy of praise, dwell on these things.

I think that through God's love, we can make a difference in this world. With His help, we can bring love and kindness to those who need it the most. Let's enjoy this season of feeling His love in a variety of ways with the people God has placed in our lives. To me, true love believes in God's word about love. For example, God declares that He loves His children with an everlasting love. Everlasting means his love lasts and endures forever. We can't make him turn his back on us. God is love on the move.

ABOUT

Dr. Willene Seaverson

Dr. Willene Owens Seaverson, PhD, is a writer, speaker, and worship leader. As a dual credit instructor at Skyline Collegiate in Dallas, Texas, Dr. Seaverson enjoys mentoring students and encouraging them to pursue their dreams. As a praise and worship leader at Fellowship Christian Center Church of Plano, where her pastor is Dr. Wayne Lee Stafford, Sr., Willene has been privileged to share her gifts internationally in St. Lucia, Kenya, Ghana, West Africa. She attended the University of Iowa for her bachelor's and master's degree and the University of North, Texas for her doctorate degree. Dr.

Seaverson enjoys spending time with her husband, Jonathan Seaverson, and spending as much time as possible with her blended family which consists of 8 children and 5 grandsons. Her gospel albums include *Godspeed*, *It's All Gonna Work Out*, *Ready for A Blessing*, and *This Christmas with Preston and Willene*.

Visit her Linktree at linktr.ee/willenemusic or e-mail Dr. Owens at willeneseaverson@gmail.com. For booking information, call 214-664-3192.

> "And we know that God causes all things to work together for good to those who love God, to those who are called according to His purpose."
>
> *Romans 8:28*

Questions to Ponder

- What does love look like to you?

- What does unconditional love look like to you?

- Which of the verses on love took you by surprise?

- Why do people believe since God loves and forgives them, they can do whatever they want? What is wrong with this kind of thinking? Is it healthy or damaging?

- How are you going to demonstrate your love for God to Him?

- What does it mean to you for God to love you no matter what you have done or how you have lived?

- Do you feel like you are worth His love, time, and attention? Why or why not?

- How is love on the move in your life? For God? For self? For others?

From Ethel Curtis

- Are you willing to take the first steps into your freedom from unforgiveness?

- What's one small thing you can do daily to show someone kindness?

From Jeannette Dixon

- Do I love yourself, and if you do, how do you demonstrate that self-love?

- How can you use God's gift of self-love to inspire and encourage yourself and others?

From Dr. Delores McLaughlin

- What love messages are you sharing with others daily?

- How deep are you willing to go to surrender your love for God, self, and others?

From Dr. Willene Seaverson

- Have you ever met anybody who experienced an unwanted pregnancy? What choice did they make? Years later, how did their decision impact them?

- Can you identify any of your former or current self-sabotaging behaviors?

A Message of Salvation to All

We are so glad that you purchased our project. As you are reading our stories, we don't want to assume that everyone reading this is a believer in God through Jesus Christ. These stories are about the love of God in the Holy Bible, and we want you to experience this same love, to the fullest.

See the four spiritual laws listed below, which is a great biblical way to connect with God through Jesus Christ and experience the love of the Bible, and so much more.

THE FOUR SPIRITUAL LAWS

 God loves you.

 We are sinful and separated from God.

 Only through Jesus Christ can you know and experience God's love and salvation.

 We must receive Jesus Christ as Savior and Lord.

1. God loves you and created you to know Him personally.

God's Love

> "For God so loved the world, that He gave His only Son, so that everyone who believes in Him will not perish, but have eternal life."
>
> *John 3:16*

God's Plan

"And this is eternal life, that they may know You, the only true God, and Jesus Christ whom You have sent." (John 17:3). What prevents us from knowing God personally?

2. Man is sinful and separated from God, so we cannot know Him personally or experience His love.

Man is Sinful

"All have sinned and fall short of the glory of God" (Romans 3:23). Man was created to have fellowship with God, but because of his own stubborn self-will, he chose to go his own independent way and fellowship with God was broken. This self-will, characterized by an attitude of active rebellion or passive indifference, is evidence of what the Bible calls sin.

Man is Separated

"The wages of sin is death" [spiritual separation from God] (Romans 6:23). "Those who do not obey the gospel of our Lord Jesus… will pay the penalty of eternal destruction, away from the presence of the Lord and from the glory of His power" (2 Thessalonians 1:8–9).

The diagram on the next page illustrates that God is holy and man is sinful. A great gulf separates the two. The arrows illustrate that man is continually trying to reach God and establish the personal relationship with Him through his own efforts, such as a good life, philosophy, or religion—but he inevitably fails. The third principle explains the only way to bridge this gulf...

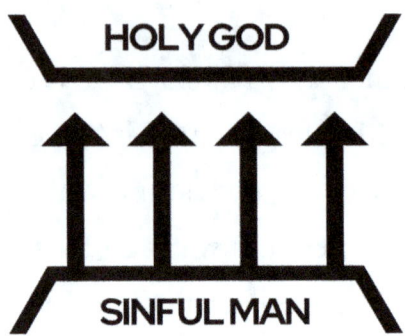

3. Jesus Christ is God's only provision for man's sin. Through Him alone we can know God personally and experience God's love.

He Died in Our Place

> "But God demonstrates His own love toward us, in that while we were still sinners, Christ died for us:"
>
> *Romans 5:8*

He Rose from the Dead

> "Christ died for our sins… He was buried… He was raised on the third day according to the Scriptures… He appeared to Cephas, then to the twelve. After that He appeared to more than five hundred…"
>
> *1 Corinthians 15:3–6*

He is the Only Way to God

> "Jesus said to him, 'I am the way, and the truth, and the life; no one comes to the Father except through Me.'"
>
> *John 14:6*

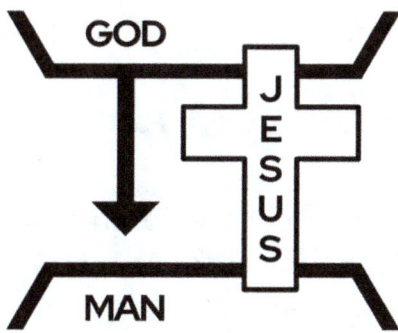

This diagram illustrates that God has bridged the gulf that separates us from Him by sending His Son, Jesus Christ, to die on the cross in our place to pay the penalty for our sins.

It is not enough just to know these truths...

4. We must individually receive Jesus Christ as Savior and Lord; then we can know God personally and experience His love.

We Must Receive Christ

> "But as many as received Him, to them He gave the right to become children of God, to those who believe in His name."
>
> *John 1:12*

We Receive Christ Through Faith

> "For by grace you have been saved through faith; and this is not of yourselves, it is the gift of God; not a result of works, so that no one may boast."
>
> *Ephesians 2:8–9*

When we receive Christ, we experience a new birth (read John 3:1–8.)

We Receive Christ by Personal Invitation

Jesus said, "Behold, I stand at the door and knock; if anyone hears My voice and opens the door, I will come in to him and will dine with him, and he with Me" (Revelation 3:20).

Receiving Christ involves turning to God from self (repentance) and trusting Christ to come into our lives to forgive us of our sins and to make us what He wants us to be. Just to agree intellectually that Jesus Christ is the Son of God and that He died on the cross for our sins is not enough. Nor is it enough to have an emotional experience. We receive Jesus Christ by faith, as an act of our will.

These two circles represent two kinds of lives:

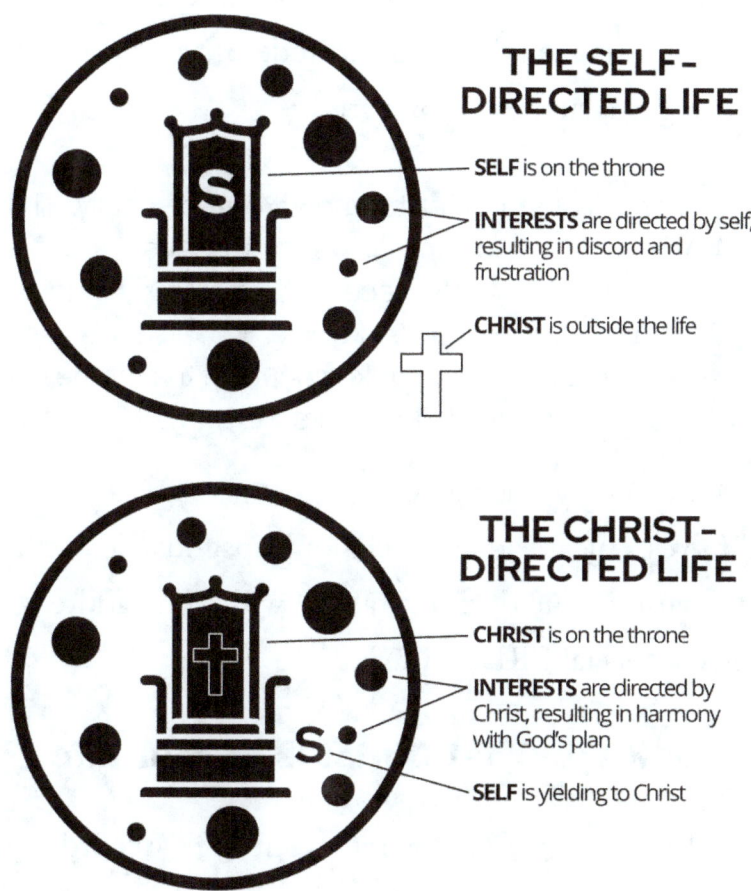

THE SELF-DIRECTED LIFE

SELF is on the throne

INTERESTS are directed by self, resulting in discord and frustration

CHRIST is outside the life

THE CHRIST-DIRECTED LIFE

CHRIST is on the throne

INTERESTS are directed by Christ, resulting in harmony with God's plan

SELF is yielding to Christ

Which circle best represents your life? Which circle would you like to have represent your life?

The following explains how you can receive Christ:

You Can Receive Christ Right Now by Faith Through Prayer

(Prayer is talking with God.)

God knows your heart and is not so concerned with your words as He is with the attitude of your heart. The following is a suggested prayer:

> "Lord Jesus, I want to know You personally. Thank You for dying on the cross for my sins. I open the door of my life and receive You as my Savior and Lord. Thank You for forgiving me of my sins and giving me eternal life. Take control of the throne of my life. Make me the kind of person You want me to be."

Did you pray this prayer?

If yes, please email relationshipsgodstyle@yahoo.com sharing your decision, along with your address, to receive a special FREE gift.

How to Know That Christ Is in Your Life

Did you receive Christ into your life? According to His promise in Revelation 3:20, where is Christ right now in relation to you? Christ said that He would come into your life and be your friend so you can know Him personally. Would He mislead you? On what authority do you know that God has answered your prayer? (The trustworthiness of God Himself and His Word.)

The Bible Promises Eternal Life to All Who Receive Christ

> "And the testimony is this, that God has given us eternal life, and this life is in His Son. The one who has the Son has the life; the one who does not have the Son of God does not have the life. These things I have written to you who believe in the name of the Son of God, so that you may know that you have eternal life."
>
> *1 John 5:11–13*

Thank God often that Christ is in your life and that He will never leave you (Hebrews 13:5). You can know based on His promise that Christ lives in you and that you have eternal life from the very moment you invite Him in. He will not deceive you.

An important reminder...

Do Not Depend on Feelings

The promise of God's Word, the Bible—not our feelings—is our authority. The Christian lives by faith (trust) in the trustworthiness of God Himself and His Word.

This train diagram illustrates the relationship among fact (God and His Word), faith (our trust in God and His Word), and feeling (the result of our faith and obedience) (John 14:21).

The train will run with or without the caboose. However, it would be useless to attempt to pull the train by the caboose. In the same way, we as Christians do not depend on feelings or emotions, but we place our faith (trust) in the trustworthiness of God and the promises of His Word.

Now That You Have Entered Into a Personal Relationship With Christ

The moment you received Christ by faith, as an act of your will, many things happened, including the following:

1. Christ came into your life (Revelation 3:20 and Colossians 1:27).
2. Your sins were forgiven (Colossians 1:14).
3. You became a child of God (John 1:12).
4. You received eternal life (John 5:24).
5. You began the great adventure for which God created you (John 10:10; 2 Corinthians 5:17 and 1 Thessalonians 5:18).

Can you think of anything more wonderful that could happen to you than entering into a personal relationship with Jesus Christ? Would you like to thank God in prayer right now for what He has done for you?

By thanking God, you demonstrate your faith.

To enjoy your new relationship with God...

Suggestions for Christian Growth

Spiritual growth results from trusting Jesus Christ. "The righteous one shall live by faith" (Galatians 3:11). A life of faith will enable you to trust God increasingly with every detail of your life, and to practice the following:

G Go to God in prayer daily (John 15:7).

R Read God's Word daily (Acts 17:11)—begin with the Gospel of John.

O Obey God moment by moment (John 14:21).

W Witness for Christ by your life and words (Matthew 4:19; John 15:8).

T Trust God for every detail of your life (1 Peter 5:7).

H Holy Spirit—Allow Him to control and empower your daily life and witness (Galatians 5:16, 17; Acts 1:8).

The Importance of Baptism

The view of most evangelical Christian scholars is that salvation is by grace through faith alone. This is especially indicated by Ephesians 2:8–9, John 3:16, 1 John 5:1. It is important to understand that baptism is a result of salvation, not a cause.

There are different baptism methods. They may include the sprinkling of water over the head of the professing believer or the total immersion of the person under water (Greek: "Baptismo" means to immerse). However, the procedure is not as important as the individual's understanding and motivation to seek baptism.

Some cite Mark 16:16 as their proof text that baptism is necessary for salvation, but they only quote the first half of the verse and typically leave out the second half, which indicates the necessity of belief as being the prerequisite to the salvation issue.

The way to resolve most problems pertaining to the issue of baptism is to look at the whole of Scripture. When we do, we find that there is absolutely nothing we can do as humans to earn salvation. Romans 6:23 tells us that salvation is a "free gift." Free means that there is nothing we can do to deserve it. On the other hand, baptism is something we choose to do. If baptism or any other human work or activity (such as going to church regularly, going on a pilgrimage, or visiting a "holy site") contributed to our salvation, we could boast that we did something and contributed to our salvation. However, Scripture says that no one should boast before God (Ephesians 2:8–9).

We come to Christ though grace by faith, and our public baptism brings glory and honor to God. Baptism is an act of obedience, not to obtain salvation, but because of it—because we love Him and want to obey Him. The motivation to pursue baptism should originate from a desire to show to the world an outward demonstration of the person's decision as well as the inward work the Holy Spirit has already begun in us. An unsaved person would not likely want to be baptized because he would not have the Holy Spirit indwelling him to prompt his desire to follow Christ in obedience (unless a sect or cult group has erroneously taught him or her otherwise). The fact that one even wants to be baptized (being assured that only faith alone in Jesus Christ saves) is evidence that the Holy Spirit already indwells that person, a result of being born of the Spirit by faith alone.

In the book of Acts, baptism is typically the outward response to coming to faith. It was seen as part of a process which includes: 1) hearing (or reading about) the gospel, 2) being convicted and led by the Holy Spirit to confess one's sins (Greek: "Homologeo" means to agree with, to speak the same), 3) coming to faith in Jesus Christ as Savior, 4) beginning the progress of growth (which includes repenting from known sin), 5) joining a group of believers or church fellowship, and 6) being baptized. The last two parts are where there are different opinions among believers or churches.

Where some churches differ with what has been stated above chiefly centers on whether a person is saved if they have not been baptized (or if they have not been baptized the "right" way). In our understanding, a person is saved when they put their faith in Christ. Of course, we all want them to join a church which exalts Christ and be baptized.

Fellowship in a Good Church

God's Word admonishes us not to forsake "our own meeting together" (Hebrews 10:25). Several logs burn brightly together; but put one aside on the cold hearth and the fire goes out. So it is with your relationship with other Christians. If you do not belong to a church, do not wait to be invited. Take the initiative; call the pastor of a nearby church where Christ is honored and His Word is preached. Start this week, and make plans to attend regularly.

The Four Spiritual Laws Written by Bill Bright.
© 1965–2013 Bright Media Foundation®